Berlitz®

Paris

Front cover: Arc de Triomphe at night

Right: Eiffel Tower

TOP 10 ATTRACTIONS

Centre Pompidou The inside-out museum showcases art from 1905 to the present day *(page 46)*

Latin Quarter and St-Germain-des-Prés The narrow streets and squares form the heart of literary Paris *(page 65)*

Eiffel Tower •
Built for the 1889 World Fair, it is still one of the most potent symbols of Paris *(page 78)*

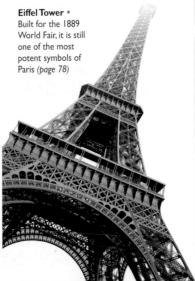

Arc de Triomphe Built to celebrate Napoleon's victories, it dominates the top of the Champs-Elysées *(page 55)*

The Louvre Once home of kings, now forum for one of the world's most outstanding collections of fine and decorative arts *(page 34)*

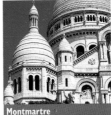

Montmartre Entertainment centre and site of Sacré-Coeur, artists have flocked to this hill for 200 years *(page 60)*

Jardin du Luxembourg Relax in the quintessential Paris park *(page 73)*

Musée d'Orsay Devoted to fine art from 1848 to 1919, notably some outstanding Impressionist works *(page 74)*

Place des Vosges One of the most elegant squares in Paris *(page 50)*

Notre-Dame A monument to Catholicism and the great Gothic architects *(page 26)*

CONTENTS

37

103

54

INTRODUCTION

The fascination of the French capital – the 'city of cities', as Victor Hugo put it – is eternal. Throughout the centuries, every new generation has added its story, and each layer is full of history and intrigue. Largely undamaged by two world wars, Paris has been created by centuries of grandiose urban planning. Its monuments and museums provoke a sense of *déjà vu*. As a result, the 'City of Light' has long been a magnet to artists, writers, philosophers and composers. According to writer Jean Giraudoux (1882–1944), the Parisian is more than a little proud to be part of a city where 'the most thinking, talking and writing in the world have been accomplished'.

Culture capital

Despite concerted attempts at decentralisation in France, Paris continues to dominate the country's art, literature, music, fashion, education, scientific research, commerce and politics.

Geography

Situated on longitude 2° 20'W and latitude 48° 50'N, roughly the same latitude as Stuttgart in Germany and Vancouver in Canada, Paris is where all the French channels of communication lead. The city itself covers an area close to 100 sq km (40 sq miles), running 13km (8 miles) east and west, and 9km (6 miles) north and south. On the map, 20 *arrondissements* (administrative districts) spiral out like a snail's shell, a pattern reflecting the city's historical development and successive enlargements.

The River Seine enters Paris close to the Bois de Vincennes in the southeast and meanders gently north and south past three small islands – the Ile St-Louis, Ile de la Cité and, on its

The view towards the Louvre's pyramid

The view from the Sacré-Coeur

way out, Ile des Cygnes. Chains of hillocks rise up to the north of the river, including Montmartre (the city's highest point), Ménilmontant, Belleville and Buttes Chaumont; and, to the south, Montsouris, the Mont Ste-Geneviève, Buttes aux Cailles and Maison Blanche.

The city is contained by the Périphérique, a ring road stretching 35km (22 miles) around it. Built in 1973 to try to reduce traffic jams, the Périphérique is invariably congested itself, particularly during rush hours, when around 150,000 cars storm its 35 exits. Forming two concentric rings wrapped tightly around Paris, the suburbs (la banlieue) are divided up into départements or counties.

At the beginning of the 19th century, Napoleon Bonaparte imposed a special status on the city of Paris, giving it the powers of a département in order to maintain a firm hold on the capital's politics and populace. Today, each arrondissement also has its own council and mayor to deal with local affairs. Nationally, Paris is represented by 21 delegates and 12 senators in the two houses of the French Parliament.

The River

'She is buffeted by the waves but sinks not,' reads the Latin inscription on the city's coat-of-arms, symbolising a Paris born on the flanks of the River Seine. Lutetia (as the city founded by the Romans was called) was established on the site of a Gallic Parisii settlement on the largest island in the river, but today it is the Seine that cuts a swathe through the middle of the city. The Seine is the capital's widest avenue; it is spanned by a total of 37 bridges, which provide some of the loveliest views of Paris.

The river is also the city's calmest thoroughfare, notwithstanding the daily flow of tourist and commercial boat traffic. In the 19th century, the banks were encumbered with wash-houses and watermills, and its waters heaved with ships from every corner of France. Even more difficult to imagine now are the 700 brightly painted Viking warships that sailed up the river to invade Paris from the north in the 9th century, or the thousands of bodies that floated past in 1572, victims of the St Bartholomew's Day Massacre, turning the Seine into a river of blood. Today, barges and pleasure boats on their way to Burgundy use the St-Martin and St-Denis canals to shorten their trip, cutting across the northeast of the city.

Paris Ambience

One of the most persistent images of Paris is one of long avenues graciously lined with chestnut and plane trees. Flowers and plants abound in a patchwork of squares, parks and gardens, tended in the formal French tradition or following the English style so admired by Napoleon III. Divided up by two large series of streets, one forming a long line north to south (from

The Montmartre café that featured in the film *Amélie*

An original Art Nouveau
Métro entrance at Abbesses

boulevard de Strasbourg to boulevard St-Michel) and the other going east to west (from rue du Faubourg-St-Antoine as far as La Défense), Paris is a mosaic of *quartiers* (quarters) or 'villages', each one having a distinctive character. Chains of boulevards encircle the centre of the city, marking where the boundary was in medieval times. Several streets contain the word *faubourg*, indicating that they were once part of the suburb outside the city wall.

The most important unofficial division in Paris is between the traditionally working-class eastern end of the city and the mostly bourgeois west. In general, the further east you go, the further left you will find yourself on the political spectrum. Rents are steep in the western *arrondissements* whereas property tends to be more affordable – for the time being – in the east. City planners have been struggling for decades to improve the balance, culminating in massive urban renewal projects at Bercy and the 'new' Left Bank *(see page 71)* in the southeast.

Population

Paris is more densely populated than Tokyo, London or New York, and the Parisians' high stress levels can be partly put down to the fact that they live literally on top of one another, squeezed into small apartments, packed into the city's 100 sq km (40 sq miles). A house and garden is an almost unheard-of luxury. There is intense competition for desirable living space, with an average of 150,000 people looking for a home at any one time. It is an oft-cited paradox that this battle for a place to live occurs in a city where 16 percent of apartments lie vacant. High rents also contribute to the fact that many Parisians have neither the time nor the money to appreciate the city they live in, being trapped in a monotonous routine they describe as *métro-boulot-dodo* (commuting, working, sleeping).

Nonetheless, for anyone fortunate enough to live in the city centre the rewards far outweigh the demands. Human in scale, clean, safe, cosmopolitan and lively, Paris lives up to its reputation as one of the best cities on earth for enjoying the good life.

Café Culture

Cafés have long played a key part in the city's intellectual, political and artistic development. Café Voltaire (1 place de l'Odéon) was where, in the 18th century, Voltaire used to meet fellow philosopher Diderot to discuss their Enlightenment theories. The 19th-century poets Verlaine and Mallarmé also conversed here, and in the 1920s the American writers Ernest Hemingway and F. Scott Fitzgerald extolled the café's 'sudden provincial quality'. Other writers in Paris between the two world wars spent hours at their favourite tables in Le Procope (13 rue de l'Ancienne-Comédie), and the Existentialist writer and philosopher Jean-Paul Sartre and his lover Simone de Beauvoir consolidated the highbrow reputation of Les Deux Magots (6 place St-Germain-des-Prés) in the 1950s. The Art Deco Café de Flore (172 boulevard St-Germain) was another of Sartre's favourites. Today, politicians congregate at Brasserie Lipp across the road.

A BRIEF HISTORY

Paris began as an island fishing community and trading port in the middle of the River Seine. Stone Age inhabitants left the earliest traces (3000BC) on the Right Bank under what is now the Louvre, but it was c.250BC before the town took form under the skilful hands of the Parisii, a Celtic tribe that settled on the Ile de la Cité.

Their island, well away from the banks of the river – much wider and more rapid than today – provided refuge from the fierce Belgae to the east. The Parisii minted their own finely crafted gold coins for trade as far afield as Britain and the Mediterranean, and the town's prosperity and strategic position attracted the attention of Julius Caesar, whose Roman legions conquered it in 52BC.

Roman stonework in the Musée National du Moyen Age

The land bordering the river was marshy (the town's ancient name Lutetia means 'marshland'), so the Romans extended inland to what is now the Left Bank's Latin Quarter. Rue St-Jacques and rue St-Martin follow the route of the old Roman road linking northern France to Orléans. Scant subterranean masonry has been found from most of the Roman buildings – forum, theatres, temples – but there are substantial remains of the public baths in what is now a wing of the Musée National du Moyen Age.

Huns and Franks overran Roman Gaul in the 3rd century, driving the citizens to retrench in the fortified Ile de la Cité – which was renamed Paris around this time. In 508, Clovis, King of the Franks, set up his court here. He later converted to Christianity, and several religious foundations date from this time – including those of the city's oldest church, St-Germain-des-Prés.

The Capetians

From 845, Norman pirates regularly raided Paris. The city stagnated until 987, when Hugues Capet, Count of Paris, became King of France. His Capetian dynasty went on to make the city the economic and political capital of France. The River Seine was once again the key to commercial prosperity, symbolised by the ship on the city's coat-of-arms with the motto *Fluctuat nec mergitur* ('She is buffeted by the waves but does not sink'). The Right Bank port area, known as the Grève, developed around the site of the present-day Hôtel de Ville.

Philippe Auguste (1180–1223) used the revenues from trade to build a fortress named the Louvre (its lower ramparts are clearly visible beneath today's museum), Notre-Dame, paved streets, aqueducts and freshwater fountains. To protect his investment while he was away on the Third Crusade, he surrounded the city with walls.

The profoundly devout, and later canonised, Louis IX (1226–70) gave the city one of its great Gothic masterpieces,

Sainte-Chapelle, and his patronage of spiritual and intellectual life gave rise to the Left Bank's Latin Quarter. From the many new schools frequented by Latin-speaking clerics, La Sorbonne university evolved, established by the king's chaplain, Robert de Sorbon. By the end of Louis's reign Paris was one of the largest cities in Western Christendom, with a population of 100,000.

In the 14th century, the city's merchant class took advantage of the political vacuum left by the devastating Black Death and the Hundred Years War with England. In 1356, with King Jean le Bon held prisoner at Poitiers, the merchants' leader, Etienne Marcel, set up a municipal government in Paris. Although he was assassinated two years later, he had shown that the Parisians were a force to be reckoned with. Wary of their militancy, Jean's successor Charles V built the Bastille fortress.

English Occupation and Religious Conflict

Civil unrest continued unabated. In 1407 the Duke of Burgundy had the Duke of Orléans murdered on rue Barbette, which led to 12 years of strife between their supporters. The Burgundians called in the help of the English, who entered Paris in 1420, following French defeat at Agincourt by England's Henry V. Ten years later, Joan of Arc tried and failed to get the English out, and in the following year came a worse humiliation: Henry VI of England was crowned King of France. But the triumph of the English was short-lived: they were soon expelled from the city, and by 1453 had lost all their French possessions except for Calais.

In the early 16th century, the city thrived under an absolutist and absent monarch, François I (1515–47), who was occupied with wars in Italy, and even imprisoned for a year in Spain. Much of the Louvre was torn down and rebuilt along the present lines. A new Hôtel de Ville (city hall) was begun, as well as the grand St-Eustache church.

The new splendour was soon bloodied by religious war, starting in 1572 with the St Bartholomew's Day massacre of 3,000 Protestants in Paris and culminating in the siege of the city by Henri de Navarre in 1589. Before the Catholic League capitulated, 13,000 Parisians had died of starvation. Henri was crowned at Chartres and finally entered the capital in 1594 – but not before having converted to Catholic himself, with the apocryphal quip that 'Paris is well worth a Mass.'

Henri IV did Paris proud once he was its master. He built the beautiful place des Vosges and place Dauphine, embellished the banks of the river with the quai de l'Arsenal, quai de l'Horloge and quai des Orfèvres, and even constructed the Samaritaine hydraulic machine that pumped fresh water to Right Bank households up until 1813. The most popular of France's monarchs, *le bon roi Henri* (good King Henry) was a notorious ladies' man. He completed the Pont-Neuf (the oldest bridge in Paris) as well as the adjacent gardens, where he was known to dally with his ladies.

The Palais de Luxembourg, built for Henri IV's widow

During the reign of Louis XIII (1610–43), Paris began to take on the fashionable aspect that became its hallmark. Elegant houses sprang up along rue du Faubourg-St-Honoré, and the magnificent *hôtels* (mansions) of the nobility were constructed in the Marais. The capital strength-ened its hold on the country with the founding of a royal printing press and Cardinal Richelieu's Académie Française.

Paris increasingly attracted nobles from the provinces – al-though too many for the liking of Louis XIV, *le Roi Soleil* ('the Sun King', 1643–1715). To bring his overly powerful and independent aristocrats into line, Louis decided to move the court out to Versailles, compelling the courtiers to live at ruinous expense in his enormous new palace.

Paris lost some of its political importance, but looked more impressive than ever, with the landscaping of the Jardin des Tuileries and the Champs-Elysées, and the building of the

Maximilien de Robespierre

Louvre's great colonnade and the Invalides hospital for wounded soldiers. The city asserted a leading cul-tural position in Europe with its new academies of the arts, literature and sciences and the establishment of the Comédie Française (1680) and several other theatres. By this time, the population had increased to 560,000.

The rumble of popular dis-content grew louder howev-er, as corruption and heavy taxes for costly foreign wars marked the reigns of the Sun King's successors, the languid Louis XV (1715–74) and the inept Louis XVI (1774–93). One of the final construction projects of the *ancien régime* was a 23-km (14-mile) wall encircling the city. Begun in 1784, it was a key factor in the subsequent unrest, for at points along the wall taxes were collected on goods brought into the city.

The Revolution

Paris was the epicentre of the political earthquake that was the French Revolution, whose aftershocks spread across France to shake up a whole continent. It had all started with protests about taxes and turned into an assault on the privileges of the monarchy, the aristocracy and the church. Middle-class intellectuals made common cause with the urban poor, the previously powerless *sans-culottes* (literally, people without breeches) to revolt. The revolutionaries destroyed the prison-fortress of the Bastille on 14 July 1789, and proceeded to execute the perceived enemies of the new republic.

A climax was reached on 21 January 1793, with the public beheading of Louis XVI. In the Reign of Terror later that year, several revolutionaries followed Louis to the guillotine: Camille Desmoulins, the fiery orator; Danton, who tried to moderate the Terror; and then the men who had organised it, Robespierre and Saint-Just.

First Empire

In 1799, Napoleon Bonaparte became first consul, and later made himself emperor. For Paris, he performed all the functions of an enthusiastic mayor, scarcely hindered by his military expeditions abroad. In Moscow, for instance, he found time to draw up statutes for the Comédie Française. Detailed maps of Paris and architectural plans for new buildings

Guillotine bridge

Masonry from the Bastille was used to build the bridge leading to what was then the place de la Révolution – now place de la Concorde – where the guillotine was erected.

Napoleon Bonaparte

were always part of his baggage. For all his spectacular monuments – the Arc de Triomphe and the column of the Grande-Armée on place Vendôme, for example – the emperor was proudest of his civic improvements: better fresh water supplies, improved drainage, new food markets and a streamlined municipal administration and police force. Most of his reforms survived long after his final defeat in 1815.

The Restoration

Although the monarchy was restored, it faced an ever-present threat in Paris from dissatisfied workers, radical intellectuals and a highly ambitious bourgeoisie. In July 1830 protest turned to riots and the building of barricades; Charles X was forced to abdicate. However, instead of restoring the republic, the revolutionary leaders played it safe and accepted the moderate Louis-Philippe or 'Citizen King'.

The Revolution of 1848, which brought Louis-Philippe's monarchy to an end, likewise started with riots and barricades in the streets of Paris. A mob threatened the royal palace, forcing the king to flee, and then invaded the Chamber of Deputies, demanding a republic. Elections followed, but they showed that however radical Paris might be, the rest of France was still largely conservative. The new National Assembly withdrew the concessions that had been made to the workers, and up went the barricades again. This time the army was called in with its heavy guns. At least 1,500 insurrectionists were killed, and thousands deported.

Second Empire

The democratically elected president, Louis-Napoleon (a nephew of Napoleon Bonaparte, whose son had died young), seized absolute power in 1851 and the following year became Emperor Napoleon III. Fear led him to modernise Paris. The insurrections of 1830 and 1848 had flared up in the densely populated working-class districts around the centre, and he wanted to prevent a recurrence. He commissioned Baron Georges Haussmann to do away with the narrow alleys that nurtured discontent, and move the occupants to the suburbs. The city was opened up with broad avenues; these so-called *grands boulevards* were too wide for barricades and gave the artillery a clear line of fire in case of revolt.

This Second Empire was a time of joyous abandon and expansion, but the emperor stumbled into war against Prussia in 1870. The army was quickly defeated, and Napoleon III's disgrace and capture brought the proclamation of a new republic, followed by a crippling Prussian siege of Paris. The city held out, albeit reduced to starvation level. When France's leaders agreed to peace, there was another uprising.

Third and Fourth Republics

The Paris Commune (self-rule by the workers) lasted 10 weeks, from 18 March to 29 May 1871, until Adolphe Thiers, the first president of the Third Republic, sent in troops from Versailles to crush it. In the last days, the *communards* set fire to the Palais des Tuileries and executed hostages, including the Archbishop of Paris. The government took revenge: at least 20,000 Commune supporters were killed in the fighting or executed later.

Prosperity rapidly returned, marked by a great construction boom. Projects begun under Napoleon III, such as the Palais-Garnier and the huge Les Halles market, were completed. The city showed off its new face at the 1889 World Fair, with the Eiffel Tower as its grandiose symbol. The splendid Métro system was inaugurated in 1900.

After this period of peace, however, two wars took their toll. The Germans failed to take Paris during World War I, but occupied it for four years (1940–44) in World War II. The city escaped large-scale bombing, and Hitler's vengeful order to destroy the city before retreating was ignored. Liberation came eventually, with a grand parade down the Champs-Elysées by General Charles de Gaulle, his Free French forces and US and British allies.

General Charles de Gaulle

The post-war city regained some of its cultural lustre under the influence of figures such as Camus, Sartre, Juliette Gréco and be-bop musicians. Under a rapid succession of governments, however, economic recovery was slow.

Fifth Republic

The Fourth Republic collapsed in 1958 after an army revolt in the colonial war in Algeria. Recalled from retirement, de Gaulle became the first president of the Fifth Republic and set about the task of restoring French prestige and morale.

From the 1968 Riots to Mitterrand's Presidency

Barricades and insurrection hit Paris again in May 1968. With workers on strike, students hurled the Latin Quarter's paving stones at the Establishment. But national elections showed that Paris was once more at odds with most of France, which voted for stability. Succeeding de Gaulle, Georges Pompidou affirmed the new prosperity with controversial riverside expressways and skyscrapers, and the striking Beaubourg cultural centre that bears his name.

In 1977 Jacques Chirac became the first democratically elected mayor of Paris in over a century. At a time when politicians could double as mayor and prime minister, Parisians benefited from leaders who furthered their national political ambitions with a dynamic municipal performance. While many questioned his taste in the shopping mall that replaced the old markets of Les Halles, Chirac is credited with the effective clean-up of the formerly dirty streets.

President François Mitterrand (1981–95) made his mark on the Paris skyline with a series of imposing works (his *grands projets*): the pyramid centrepiece of the reorganised Louvre, the Grande Arche de La Défense, the Opéra Bastille, the Institut du Monde Arabe and the national library that bears his name.

Family Values

France's birthrate of 1.9 children per family exceeds the European average but is still a source of concern for the state. Every *famille nombreuse* (ie with three children or more) is rewarded with benefits including nursery provision, subsidised public transport, car tax and school meals, as well as free admission to museums. In 2004 the population of France reached 60 million, overtaking that of the UK (at 59 million). The birthrate has been boosted by France's large Muslim community, whose numbers are, according to many demographers, steadily rising.

Paris Today

After a 20-year campaign, Chirac left the mayor's job to become president in 1995. Within two years, however, his popularity had dwindled, and Lionel Jospin, from the opposing Socialist Party, became prime minister. Their period of joint stewardship was one of economic growth, reduced unemployment and rising property values.

Nicolas Sarkozy

In the 2001 mayoral elections, Parisians voted for Bertrand Delanoë, the city's first socialist mayor for 130 years and the first openly gay mayor in France. However, the first round of the 2002 presidential elections saw a huge resurgence of the right, in which the National Front candidate Jean-Marie Le Pen beat Jospin. Though Chirac went on to beat Le Pen in the second round, the degree of support for Le Pen shocked governments all over Europe.

Parisians took to the streets to express their rejection of Le Pen; they contributed massively to Chirac's second round victory on 5 May 2002. President Chirac then led a determined opposition to the war in Iraq, which saw his approval ratings at home soar, only to plummet after initiating reforms to the state pension and benefit system. By 2007, he was widely regarded as a spent force. His party's candidate to succeed him, Nicolas Sarkozy, won the presidency in May and has promised sweeping economic and social reforms. As the country continues to face the challenges of the 21st century, many believe that it is still striving to quell its revolutionary spirit and become a cohesive nation at ease with itself.

Historical Landmarks

c250BC Celtic settlement on island in the River Seine.

52BC Roman conquest, followed by expansion to Left Bank.

508 Clovis, King of Franks, makes Paris his capital.

987 Hugues Capet elected King of France.

1420 The English occupy Paris.

1431 Henry VI of England crowned King of France.

1436 English expelled.

1594 Henri IV enters Paris.

1682 Louis XIV moves court to Versailles.

1789 Storming of Bastille starts French Revolution.

1793 Execution of Louis XVI and Marie-Antoinette; Reign of Terror.

1804 Napoleon Bonaparte becomes emperor.

1814–15 Fall of Napoleon; restoration of Bourbon monarchy.

1830 Bourgeois revolution; Louis-Philippe, the Citizen King.

1848 Revolution brings Louis-Napoleon to power.

1870–1 Franco-Prussian War; Second Empire ends; Paris besieged.

1871 Paris Commune – 10 weeks of workers' rule.

1900 First Métro line opened.

1914–18 World War I. Germans advance to within eight miles of Paris.

1939 World War II begins.

1940 French government capitulates; Germans occupy Paris.

1944 Free French and other Allied forces liberate Paris.

1958 Fall of Fourth Republic. De Gaulle becomes president.

1968 Student riots, workers' general strikes.

1977 Jacques Chirac becomes first elected mayor since 1871.

1981–95 President Mitterrand's new building includes Louvre Pyramid.

1995 Jacques Chirac elected president.

2002 The euro replaces the franc as France's unit of currency.

2003 In August, nearly 15,000 people die in a heatwave.

2005 Urban unrest in the capital over immigration and racism.

2006 Controversial youth employment law sparks protests in Paris.

2007 Nicolas Sarkozy elected president.

WHERE TO GO

Paris is an easy city to navigate. Much of it is easily covered on foot, and it has efficient bus and Métro systems. The biggest divide is between the Rive Droite (Right Bank) and Rive Gauche (Left Bank) on either side of the river Seine, which cuts through the heart of the city. Each Bank has its own connotations: the Right as the business and commercial powerhouse; the Left as the place for intellectuals and learning. There is also an east-west divide between traditionally wealthy western Paris and poorer eastern Paris. But these divisions have their nuances: arty centres of creation are now more likely to be in northeast Paris than affluent, unaffordable St-Germain-des-Prés, and young urban professionals are increasingly buying into the affordable, traditionally working-class districts.

Administratively, the city is divided into 20 *arrondissements*, starting with the 1st in the centre (taking in part of Ile de la Cité and the area around the Louvre) and spiralling outwards clockwise to end at the 20th in the northeast. Confusingly, while Parisians often refer to the *arrondissement* in which they live, they also refer to the historic *quartiers*, such as the Marais, St-Germain, Bastille or Latin Quarter, that on occasions straddle *arrondissements* (the Marais, for example, extends into the 3rd and the 4th *arrondissements*; the Latin Quarter into the 5th and the 6th).

Opposite: soaring Eiffel Tower
Right: Métro sign

Notre-Dame and the eastern end of the Ile de la Cité

ILE DE LA CITÉ

During the 3rd century BC, the Celtic tribe of the Parisii built their first huts on the Ile de la Cité, the largest island in the Seine. In 52BC, Roman legions conquered the settlement and founded Lutetia Parisiorum on the left bank. During the Middle Ages, the island was the centre of political, religious and judicial power, not only for Paris but for the whole of France. Nowadays, the island is still the geographical centre of the capital and home to several of the city's main official buildings. Sainte-Chapelle and Notre-Dame make the island an enduring focus for religious tourism in the city.

Notre-Dame

Dominating the island is **Notre-Dame** (open daily 7.45am–6.45pm, tel: 01 42 34 56 10, visits restricted during services, <www.cathedraledeparis.com>). The cathedral has played a religious role for at least 2,000 years. In Roman times a temple to Jupiter stood here; in the 4th century AD a Christian church, St-Etienne, was built on the site; this was joined two centuries later by a second church, dedicated to the Virgin. Norman raids left them both in a sorry state, and, in the 12th century, Bishop Maurice de Sully decided that a cathedral should be built to replace them.

The main part of Notre-Dame, begun in 1163, took 167 years to finish. Its transition from Romanesque to Gothic has been called a perfect representation of medieval architecture – an opinion that has attracted dissenters both ancient and modern. Cistercian monks protested that such a sumptuous structure was an insult to the godly virtue of poverty, and today many architectural purists still find Notre-Dame excessive.

The original architect is unknown, but Pierre de Montreuil (who was involved in the building of Sainte-Chapelle, *see page 30*) was responsible for much of the 13th-century work. The present look of the cathedral is due to Eugène Viollet-le-Duc, who from 1845 to 1863 restored it following the ravages of the 18th century, caused more by pre-Revolutionary meddlers than by revolutionaries who stripped it of religious symbols.

Popular support for the expensive restoration was inspired by Victor Hugo's novel *Notre-Dame de Paris*.

Notre-Dame's rose window

The cathedral has witnessed numerous momentous occasions over the centuries, including, in 1239, the procession of Louis IX, during which the pious king walked barefoot, carrying his holy treasure – believed to be Christ's crown of thorns. In 1594 Henri IV made his politically motivated conversion to Catholicism here to reinforce his hold on the French throne. Napoleon crowned himself emperor at Notre-Dame, upstaging the Pope, who had come to Paris expecting to do it; the scene is depicted in Jacques-Louis David's vast painting, *The Consecration of Napoleon,* now in the Louvre. More recent occasions include General de Gaulle marking the 1944 Liberation of Paris with a Mass here, and in 1970 his death was also commemorated here.

The West Front

Across the three doorways of the west front, the 28 statues of the **Galerie des Rois** represent the kings of Judah. These are 19th-century restorations: the originals were torn down during the Revolution because they were thought to depict kings of France (21 of them were recently discovered and

Notre-Dame's magnificent Gothic west front

moved to the Musée du Moyen Age, *see page 67*).

The central **rose window** depicts the Redemption after the Fall. Two more outsized rose windows illuminate the transept; the northern one retains most of its 13th-century glass. A 14th-century *Virgin and Child* is to the right of the choir entrance.

The 255-step climb up the **north tower** (open daily Oct–Mar 10am–4.45pm, Apr–Sept 9am–6.45pm, <www.monuments-nationaux.fr>) is rewarded with glorious views of Paris and close-ups of the roof and Notre-Dame's famous gargoyles. Cross over to the south tower – and another 122 steps – to see the 13-ton bell, the only one still remaining (the Revolutionaries melted down the others to make cannons). The bell was re-cast in the 1680s. A further 124 steps lead to the top of the south tower for more spectacular views.

Napoleon III's town planner Baron Haussmann *(see page 19)* greatly enlarged the *parvis*, or cathedral forecourt, diminishing the impact of the towering west front. Excavations beneath the square have revealed walls and foundations from the Gallic, Roman and medieval eras, which now form part of an exhibition on early Paris.

War memorial

Behind Notre-Dame is the Mémorial des Martyrs de la Déportation, a reminder of the 200,000 French who died in concentration camps during World War II. A dark staircase leads down to a crypt (open daily 10am–noon, 2–5pm, until 7pm in summer), where the names of deportees are inscribed on the walls.

Palais de la Cité

The other architectural and historical highlight on the Ile de la Cité is the **Palais de la Cité**, the complex of buildings that includes the Conciergerie, Sainte-Chapelle and the Palais de Justice, the headquarters of the French supreme court.

Bars at the Conciergerie

Palais de Justice

The imposing neoclassical **Palais de Justice** (open Mon–Sat 1.30–6pm, <www.ca-paris.justice.fr>), heart of the French legal system, stands on the site of the Roman palace where Emperor Julian was crowned in AD360. The lobby (Salle des Pas Perdus) is well worth a visit to catch a glimpse of the lawyers, plaintiffs, witnesses, court reporters and hangers-on waiting for the wheels of French justice to grind into action.

Conciergerie

Adjacent is the **Conciergerie** (open daily Mar–Oct 9.30am–6pm, Nov–Feb 9am–4.30pm, <www.monuments-nationaux.fr>), originally the residence of the king's concierge. The 'medieval' facade dates from the 1850s. The building's notoriety, however, dates from the late 18th century: in 1793, at the height of the Terror, the Conciergerie became the antechamber of the guillotine, with around 2,500 condemned spending their last night here *(see page 17)*. It is now a museum to its bloody past, displaying items including a guillotine blade, the crucifix before which Marie-Antoinette prayed while captive here, and the lock used on Robespierre's cell. Look out on the Cour des Femmes, where husbands, wives and lovers were allowed a final tryst before the tumbrels came to carry off the prisoners.

Sainte-Chapelle

Concealed in the courtyard between the Palais de Justice and the Conciergerie is the magnificent Gothic **Sainte-Chapelle** (open daily Mar–Oct, 9.30am–6pm, Nov–Feb 9am–5pm, <www.monuments-nationaux.fr>). The chapel was constructed in 1248 to designs by Pierre de Montreuil to house holy relics, fragments of which were believed to be Christ's Crown of Thorns, bought by pious King Louis IX (later St-Louis). The lower chapel, with its star-patterned ceiling, was used by palace servants. More impressive is the upper level, where light blazes through 15-m (3¼-ft) high glass windows separated by buttresses so slim that there seems to be no wall at all. Of the 1,134 individual pieces of glass, 720 are 13th-century originals.

Between 1789 and 1815 Sainte-Chapelle served various roles: as a flour warehouse in the Revolution, as a club for high-ranking dandies, then as an archive for Napoleon's Consulate. This latter role fortunately saved the chapel from projected destruction, since the bureaucrats could not think of another site in which to keep their mountains of paper.

Sainte-Chapelle's lower chapel

Other Attractions on the Ile de la Cité

At the western end of the island is the pretty, tree-shaded **square du Vert-Galant** and, beyond it, a statue of Henri IV and the recently cleaned **Pont-Neuf**, which, despite its name – meaning 'New Bridge' – is actually the oldest bridge in Paris. Its survival is due to the fact that it is made of stone, rather than wood, and also because it was the first bridge in Paris to be constructed without houses on it. In 1985, the Pont-Neuf hit the headlines when Bulgarian-born American artist Christo wrapped the entire structure in fabric.

You can return to the eastern end of the island via the colourful **Marché aux Fleurs** on place Louis Lépine, opposite the Préfecture de Police and Hôtel Dieu. The latter, now a city hospital, was built on the site of a medieval hospital; it was the scene of intense battles when the police resisted the Germans in 1944. In contrast to these forbidding structures, the market is an array of small glasshouses selling flowers and plants. On Sunday, the stalls become a market for caged birds.

ILE ST-LOUIS

The pedestrianised Pont St-Louis leads from the Ile de la Cité to the **Ile St-Louis**, an island renowned for its elegant, exclusive and astronomically expensive mansions. From the western end of the shady quai d'Orléans (at the western end of the island) there is a wonderful view of the apse of Notre-Dame. However, some pilgrims to this spot are more intent on a visit to another Parisian institution: ice-cream parlour **Berthillon** (open Wed–Sun 10am–8pm), at 29–31 rue St-Louis-en-l'Ile, the street that cuts through the island. It's a pretty road, dotted with boutiques and restaurants. Towards the eastern end is the baroque church of **St-Louis-en-l'Ile**, notable for its fine collection of Dutch, Flemish and Italian 16th- and 17th-century art.

The mansions of the Ile St-Louis and beyond

On the northeastern end of the island, at 17 quai d'Anjou, is the grand **Hôtel Lauzun**, built in 1640 by Louis Le Vau, architect to Louis XIV, and now owned by the Rothschild family. It was here that the poets Théophile Gautier and Charles Baudelaire lived in 1845, and where Baudelaire wrote part of *Les Fleurs du Mal*. In the **Hôtel Lambert**, on the corner of rue St-Louis-en-l'Ile, Voltaire once enjoyed a tempestuous love affair with the lady of the house, the Marquise du Châtelet.

On the island's south bank is the small **Musée Adam Mickiewicz** (open by reservation only Thur 2.15–5.45pm, tel: 01 55 42 83 88). A Polish poet, Mickiewicz (1798–1855) lived in Paris from 1832 to 1840 and devoted himself to helping oppressed Poles. The 17th-century building in which the museum is housed also includes the Polish Library and displays memorabilia of the Polish composer Frédéric Chopin.

Old and new at the Louvre

THE LOUVRE, TUILERIES & CONCORDE

Palais du Louvre

Eight centuries in the making, but with great architectural harmony nonetheless, the **Louvre** was originally built as a fortress by Philippe Auguste in 1190. When Louis XIV moved his court to Versailles, he abandoned the Louvre to artists and other squatters. The Revolutionaries made it a public museum in 1793. As the home of the *Mona Lisa,* the Louvre drew almost unmanageable crowds, until President Mitterrand ordered its re-organisation in the 1980s. A vast new reception area was excavated and topped by the glass **Pyramid** by Sino-American architect I.M. Pei, now the main entrance.

Musée du Louvre

The **Musée du Louvre** (open Wed–Mon 9am–6pm, Wed and Fri until 10pm, closed public holidays, tickets are valid all day and allow re-entry into the museum, tel: 01 40 20 50 50, <www.louvre.fr>) is divided into three wings: Richelieu in the north, Sully in the east and Denon in the south. The collections are spread over differently colour-coded sections, to facilitate orientation. An excellent map to help with this is available at the ticket desks.

The following is a brief summary of the Louvre's many treasures, including information on the highlights from the various different sections.

Lower-Ground and Ground Floors

A good place to start from is the exhibition on the medieval Louvre, on the lower-ground floor of the Sully Wing. This is where the remains of Philippe-Auguste's fort and keep, and some of the artefacts discovered in excavations in the 1980s, can be seen. Above, on the ground floor of the Sully Wing, are Egyptian and Greek Antiquities, while on the ground floor of the Denon wing are Etruscan and Roman Antiquities including the *Sarcophagus of a Married Couple* and a *Borghese Gladiator,* and Italian sculpture such as Michelangelo's *Dying Slave* and Canova's neoclassical *Psyche and Cupid* (1793).

Making the Most of the Museums

Entry charges for museums range from around €5–12, with reduced rates for children, students and pensioners. Some museums charge less on Sunday, and entrance is always free on the first Sunday of the month for the following: the Louvre, Musée d'Orsay, Centre Pompidou, Musée de l'Orangerie, Musée Rodin, Musée Picasso and Musée du Moyen Age. The **Paris Museum Pass** (<www.parismuseumpass.fr>) gives entry to over 60 museums and monuments in Paris and its surroundings, including the Louvre and Versailles. You can buy passes valid for two, four or six consecutive days at museums, tourist offices and Métro stations.

The lower ground floor of the Richelieu Wing showcases French sculpture, including Guillaume Coustou's giant *Horses of Marly*. On the ground floor of Richelieu, the French sculpture collection continues, with works spanning the 5th to 18th centuries. Also here are Mesopotamian finds such as the black basalt Babylonian *Code of Hammurabi* (1792–1750BC), one of the world's first legal documents.

First Floor

The first floor is where some of the biggest crowd-pullers are housed. On the first floor of the Denon Wing is a spectacular collection of large-format French painting, notably Delacroix's *Liberty Leading the People*, Géricault's *Raft of the Medusa* and David's *Consecration of Napoleon*. Adjacent is a room showcasing Leonardo da Vinci's enigmatic Florentine noblewoman, the *Mona Lisa (La Joconde)*. This iconic

Delacroix's *Liberty Leading the People*

piece, painted in 1503, hangs alongside Veronese's vast *Wedding at Cana* and other masterpieces from the Venetian Renaissance.

Leonardo's *Mona Lisa*

At the staircase dividing the Denon and Sully wings is the *Winged Victory of Samothrace* (2nd century BC), a Hellenistic figurehead commemorating a victory at sea, and the glittering Galerie d'Apollon (Apollo's Gallery), home to the crown jewels. At this point you reach the Sully Wing and the graceful Hellenic statue of the *Venus de Milo* (2nd century BC), bought by the French government for 6,000 francs in 1820 from the island of Milos. Most of the first floor of the Richelieu Wing houses works of the decorative arts.

Second Floor
The whole second floor is dedicated to painting, with highlights including Dürer's *Self-Portrait*, Vermeer's *The Lacemaker,* Watteau's *Pierrot* and Ingres's *The Turkish Bath*. The Richelieu Wing houses works from Flanders, the Netherlands, Germany and France (14th to 17th centuries); the second floor of the Sully Wing is devoted to French paintings of the 17th, 18th and 19th centuries.

Additional Museums
In a separate wing are three other collections (entrance at 107 rue de Rivoli, all open Tues–Fri 11am–6pm, Sat–Sun 10am–6pm). The **Musée des Arts Décoratifs** presents a survey of

interior design, from medieval tapestries to 21st-century design. The **Musée des Arts de la Mode et du Textile** covers Paris fashions and textiles from the 16th century to the present, and, upstairs, the **Musée de la Publicité** is home to a rich collection of posters from the Middle Ages to the present.

Palais-Royal

The **Palais-Royal**, located directly north of the Louvre, across rue de Rivoli, was built in 1639 as Cardinal Richelieu's residence. It gained its regal title when Anne of Austria moved in with young Louis XIV. This serene, arcaded palace has a colourful past. In the days of Philippe d'Orléans, Prince Regent while Louis XV was a child, it was the scene of notorious orgies. A later duke (another Philippe) added apartments above the arcades, along with two theatres (one now the Comédie Française, *see page 94*), shops, gambling houses and fashionable cafés.

Arcades of the Palais-Royal

Despite efforts to curry favour with the revolutionaries, such as calling himself Philippe Egalité (equality), the duke ended up on the guillotine with the rest of the family. After the Revolution, the palace became a gambling den again and narrowly escaped destruction during the 1871 uprising. Following restoration (1872–6), however, it regained respectability.

It now houses the Ministry of Culture, the Council of State, the Constitutional Council, some shops and the historic Grand Véfour restaurant *(see page 136)*.

Near the Palais-Royal

East of the Palais-Royal is the **Banque de France**, while just north is the **Bibliothèque Nationale Richelieu** (National Library, open Mon 2–8pm, Tues–Thur 10am–8pm, Sun 10am–7pm, tel: 01 53 79 53 79, <www.bnf.fr>). The latter became a royal library in 1368, when Charles V placed 973 manuscripts in the Louvre. Most of the millions of books, engravings and ancient manu-

Cour d'Honneur

In 1986, artist Daniel Buren installed rows of black-and-white-striped stone columns in the Palais-Royal's main quadrangle, the Cour d'Honneur.

scripts it has accumulated over the centuries have been transferred to the newer national library on the Left Bank *(see page 71)*. The old building with its splendid reading room (1863) has been transformed into a specialist research library.

The Tuileries

West of the Louvre is the one of the city centre's main green spaces, the **Jardin des Tuileries** (open daily Mar–Sept 7am–9pm, Oct–Feb 7.30am–7pm), named after a 13th-century tile works and beautifully landscaped according to plans by André Le Nôtre. Walk around the chestnut and lime trees, and admire sculptor Aristide Maillol's sensual statues of nymphs and

Relaxing in the Tuileries, with Concorde's Obelisk in view

languorous maidens, a few of which are coquettishly half concealed behind a miniature maze. The gardens' 28 hectares (69 acres) extend across the site of the royal Palais des Tuileries, burnt down during the 1871 Commune *(see page 19)*.

At the eastern entrance to the Tuileries is the pink **Arc de Triomphe du Carrousel**, built at roughly the same time as the Arc de Triomphe *(see page 55)*. The latter is visible from here in a straight line beyond the Obelisk on place de la Concorde. The same axis continues into the distant haze to the skyscrapers of La Défense.

Jeu de Paume and Musée de l'Orangerie
A few fragments of the Palais des Tuileries can be seen by the **Jeu de Paume**, in the northwest corner of the gardens. Once home to real-tennis courts (hence the name) and, later, to the collection of Impressionist paintings now displayed at the Musée d'Orsay *(see page 74)*, the building is currently the attractive showcase for the **Centre National de la Photographie** (open Tues noon–9pm, Wed–Fri noon–7pm, Sat, Sun 10am–7pm, <www.jeudepaume.org>). The centre is the showcase for changing exhibitions on all photographic disciplines, including major fashion retrospectives and contemporary video installations.

In the southwestern corner of the Tuileries is the **Musée de l'Orangerie** (open Wed–Mon 12.30–7pm, Fri until 9pm, <www.musee-orangerie.fr>). The building was constructed as a hothouse by Napoleon III, but, since the 1920s, has been the showcase for eight of Claude Monet's water-lily paintings, in which the Impressionist painter captured the play of colour on the pond in his Japanese garden at Giverny *(see page 86)* at different times of day. Extensively renovated and reopened in 2006, the two vast oval rooms upstairs show off the paintings as specified by Monet. In the gallery space downstairs is the Jean Walter and Paul Guillaume Collection, an exceptional array of works by artists including Cézanne, Renoir, Matisse, Picasso, Soutine, Modigliani, Utrillo and Henri Rousseau.

Place de la Concorde

Jacques-Ange Gabriel designed the vast **place de la Concorde** as place Louis XV in 1753, but the Revolutionaries dispensed with all royal connotations. The King's statue was replaced with a guillotine, used to behead Louis XVI and over 1,000 other victims. In 1934, the square was the scene of bloody anti-government rioting by French fascists.

In the centre of the square is a pink-granite, 23-m (75-ft) tall Obelisk, a gift from Mohammed Ali, viceroy of Egypt. Dating from 1300BC and once part of the temple of Ramses II in Luxor, it was erected here in 1836.

The two horses guarding the entrance to the Champs-Elysées *(see page 54)* are replicas of the 18th-century *Horses of Marly*, sculpted by Guillaume Coustou (originals in the Louvre, *see page 36*).

Death toll

According to official estimates, 1,119 people were decapitated on place de la Concorde, including Louis XVI, his queen Marie-Antoinette, Charlotte Corday, the poet André Chénier and, ironically, even Revolutionary leader Robespierre.

THE GRANDS BOULEVARDS

North of the Louvre and Tuileries are the Grand Boulevards, a line of wide avenues running from west to east. The boulevards date from the 17th century, when Louis XIV tore down the medieval walls around Paris and created broad, tree-lined spaces. In the 19th century Baron Haussmann extended the string westwards, and the western end of what was named boulevard Haussmann became the preserve of the rich. Today stretches of the central boulevards are dominated by high-street clothing chains, although traces of the Second Empire extravagance can still be seen in the ornate balconies and facades.

Palais Garnier

Soaring over the place de l'Opéra is the city's historic opera house, the **Palais Garnier** (open daily 10am–5pm, guided

Galeries Lafayette on boulevard Haussmann

tours in English Tues–Sun at 1pm and 2pm, tel: 01 40 01 22 63, <www.operadeparis.fr>), which puts on opera and ballet in tandem with the newer Opéra Bastille *(see page 52)*.

In 1860 architect Charles Garnier was commissioned by Napoleon III to build an opera house, and his lavish designs were in tune with the pomp and opulence that characterised the Second Empire. The five-tiered auditorium, dripping with velvet and gilt,

Chagall ceiling, Palais Garnier

is dominated by a vast chandelier, which crashed down on the audience during a performance in 1896. The auditorium ceiling was painted by Marc Chagall in 1964. Tours also take in the library and museum, showcasing scores, costumes and sets.

Madeleine

A stock exchange, the Bank of France, a theatre: these were among the uses proposed for the huge neoclassical church of **La Madeleine** (open daily 9am–7pm), at the heart of place de la Madeleine. Napoleon wanted it as a temple of glory for his army, but his architect suggested the Arc de Triomphe for that use instead. The restored monarchy opted to use the Madeleine as a church, and the building was finally consecrated in 1842. Climb the steps for great views down rue Royale to place de la Concorde and the Assemblée Nationale.

Place de la Madeleine is also home to luxury shops, including Fauchon (nicknamed 'millionaire's supermarket'), Hédiard chocolatiers and truffle retailers Maison de la Truffe. Also on the square is the Kiosk-Théâtre de la Madeleine, where you can buy half-price seats for same-day theatre shows across Paris.

Musée Jacquemart-André

Not far from the Madeleine, at 158 boulevard Haussmann, is the **Musée Jacquemart-André** (open daily 10am–6pm, <www.musee-jacquemart-andre.com>). The museum displays art and furniture that once belonged to wealthy collector Edouard André and his wife, erstwhile society portrait painter Néllie Jacquemart. The house is magnificent, and its fine-art collection includes works by Bellini, Boucher, David, Donatello, Uccello, Rembrandt and Titian. The gorgeous café, decorated with chandeliers and antiques, is also worth a visit.

Place Vendôme

Louis XIV wanted this square to be an imposing setting for a monument to him, but, after it was laid out in 1699, only his financiers could afford the rent. Today the Ministry of Justice shares the square with banks, famous jewellers and the Ritz hotel. The statue of Louis XIV was overthrown during the Revolution, and its replacement, the Vendôme column, commemorates the victories of Napoleon, cast from 1,250 Austrian cannons captured at Austerlitz and topped by a statue of the emperor. Like him, it was toppled, in the 1871 Commune (see page 19) at the instigation of painter Gustave Courbet, who had to pay the crippling cost of having it re-erected two years later.

Jewellers on place Vendôme

The inside-out Centre Pompidou

BEAUBOURG, LES HALLES & THE MARAIS

Sandwiched between the Louvre and Palais-Royal to the west and the Marais to the east, Beaubourg and Les Halles form one of the city's busiest commercial and cultural centres. The biggest landmark is the Centre Pompidou, Paris's modern art museum. The Marais is an elegant, characterful district, with fine mansions, museums, attractive boutiques, kosher grocers, gay bars and cosy cafés bundled together in a labyrinth of narrow streets.

Châtelet and Hôtel de Ville

Place du Châtelet is a good starting point for exploring the area. Flanked by two theatres (Théâtre de la Ville and Théâtre du Châtelet), the square lies above one of Paris's biggest Métro and RER stations.

Opening out at the eastern end of avenue Victoria is the wide esplanade of the **Hôtel de Ville** (open Mon–Sat ◀

10am–7pm), the ornate home of the city council. The neo-Renaissance building, with its magnificent Mansard roof, was rebuilt after the 17th-century town hall was destroyed by fire in the 1871 Commune *(see page 19)*. In medieval times, place de l'Hôtel de Ville was the site of hangings and executions, but today, the pedestrianised square is considerably more alluring, especially in the evening, when the fountains are floodlit.

Centre Pompidou

'That'll get them screaming,' said then-President Georges Pompidou, as he approved the plans for the cultural centre bearing his name, but more popularly known as Beaubourg, after its 13th-century neighbourhood. The **Centre Georges-Pompidou** (open Wed–Mon 11am–8pm, Thur and for some exhibitions until 10pm, <www.centrepompidou.fr>) was

Georges, the swish restaurant on top of the Centre Pompidou

built by architects Richard Rogers, Renzo Piano and Gianfranco Franchini, and its inside-out design, dominated by external pipes, tubes, scaffolds and escalators, caused controversy when unveiled in 1977. The pipes are not just for show: the blue ones convey air, the green ones carry water, the yellow ones contain the electrics, and the red ones conduct heating. The

Stravinsky Fountain

building houses a cinema, library, design centre, music 'laboratory' and museum. The plaza outside is a popular rendezvous point and the site of the Stravinsky Fountain, featuring colourful sculptures by Niki de Saint Phalle.

The **Musée National d'Art Moderne** (National Museum of Modern Art) is housed on the fourth and fifth floors (fifth floor closed for renovation until 2007; until then a selection of both modern and contemporary works is showing on the fourth floor). Highlights of the modern period, from 1905 to the 1960s, include works by Kandinsky, Klee, Klein, Matisse, Picasso and Pollock, and sections on Dadaism and Surrealism. The centre's contemporary collection, incorporating work from the 1960s to the present day, includes pieces by Andy Warhol, Verner Panton, Joseph Beuys, Gerhard Richter and Jean Dubuffet. On level six are temporary exhibitions and the fashionable, minimalist – and expensive – Georges restaurant.

Included within the price of the ticket to the Musée National d'Art Moderne is a visit to a reconstruction of sculptor Constantin Brancusi's studio, Atelier Brancusi (open Wed–Mon 2–6pm).

Statue at St-Eustache

Les Halles

For centuries this was the site of the capital's main food markets (now located out of town, near Orly), but, to widespread regret, the iron-and-glass pavilions were demolished in 1971. Gardens, playgrounds and the partly subterranean, much disliked, shopping centre, **Forum des Halles**, have taken their place.

Near Les Halles is the Renaissance **Fontaine des Innocents**, once part of a cemetery but now a popular meeting spot. Bars and restaurants line the adjoining rue Berger and the streets leading off it. Away from the gardens and playgrounds, the quarter has its seedy side: drink and drugs, pickpockets and prostitutes. Rue St-Denis, once primarily a red-light district, is now pedestrianised, but still has a number of sex shops.

The church of **St-Eustache** dominates the north side of Les Halles. Built from 1532 to 1637, the main structure is late Gothic with an imposing Renaissance colonnade on its western façade. The church is renowned for its concerts.

The Marais

This district, to the north of the Ile de la Cité and Ile St-Louis, has successfully withstood the onslaught of modern construction. It provides a remarkably authentic record of the development of the city, from the reign of Henri IV at the end of the 16th century to the advent of the Revolution. Built on reclaimed marshland, as its name suggests (*marais* is the French for 'swamp'), the **Marais** contains some of Europe's most elegant Renaissance mansions *(hôtels)*, many of which now serve as museums and libraries. In the 1960s, the government designated the area an historical monument, and conservation and restoration took hold. The big change in recent years has been the influx of trendy boutiques and gay bars.

Take the Métro to Rambuteau and start at the corner of rue des Archives and rue des Francs-Bourgeois, named after the poor (not bourgeois at all) who were allowed to live here tax-free in the 14th century. The national archives are stored in an 18th-century mansion, the **Hôtel de Soubise** (open Mon, Wed–Fri 10am–12.30pm, 2–5.30pm, Sat–Sun 12–5.30pm). Across a vast, horseshoe-shaped courtyard, you come across the rococo style of Louis XV's time in the apartments of the Prince and Princess of Soubise.

The elegant Hôtel Carnavalet

Marais Museums

The Marais is home to a number of prestigious museums, including, on rue des Francs-Bourgeois, the grand **Musée Carnavalet** (open Tue–Sun 10am–6pm, <www.carnavalet.paris.fr>), which charts the history of the city of Paris. The museum is housed in the magnificent Hôtel Carnavalet, which was once home to the lady of letters Madame de Sévigné. The building's present name

Le Petit Fer à Cheval, on
rue du Vieille-du-Temple

comes from the distortion of the name of former owner Françoise de Kernevenoy.

The splendid **Musée National Picasso** (open Wed–Mon 9.30am–5.30pm, until 6pm in summer, <www.musee-picasso.fr>), nearby at 5 rue Thorigny, is set within the restored Hôtel Salé (the name *salé*, meaning 'salty', derives from the salt tax once levied by its former owner). On display are more than 200 paintings, 158 sculptures and hundreds of drawings, engravings, ceramics and models for stage sets and costumes drawn from the artist's personal collection, as well as works by Braque, Matisse, Miró, Degas, Renoir and Rousseau collected by Picasso.

Another Marais museum, housed in the Hôtel Donon at 8 rue Elzévir, is the **Musée Cognacq-Jay** (open Tues–Sun 10am–6pm), which contains a splendid collection of 18th-century paintings, furniture and *objets d'art*, bequeathed to the city by the founders of La Samaritaine. This grand old department store (at Châtelet), known for its impressive Art Deco interior, is currently closed for major safety improvements.

Place des Vosges

Rue des Francs-Bourgeois ends at what many agree is the most attractive residential square in Paris, **place des Vosges** (originally place Royale). Henri IV had it laid out in 1605 on the site of an old horse-market, the idea being to have 'all the houses in the same symmetry'. After the wedding festivities of his son Louis XIII, the gardens became the fashionable place to promenade, and, later, a spot for aristocratic duels.

The Romantic writer Victor Hugo lived at No. 6, now a **museum** (open Tues–Sun 10am–6pm) housing a small collection of his artefacts. It's primarily worth a visit to see the interior of one of the square's grand mansions.

Jewish Quarter

Rue des Rosiers is the hub of what remains of the Jewish quarter. As the Marais has become popular with bar and boutique owners, the Jewish community has retreated to a small pocket centred on this narrow street lined with kosher delis and falafel stands. Jewish history is detailed at the **Musée d'Art et d'Histoire du Judaïsme** (open Mon–Fri 11am–6pm, Sun 10am–6pm) on rue du Temple. The **synagogue**, with its Art Nouveau facade by Hector Guimard, is at 4 rue Pavée.

Place des Vosges

BASTILLE & EASTERN PARIS

For years a run-down area, Bastille was given a shot in the arm by the construction of a new opera house in the late 20th century. The area south of here has since become a potent symbol of urban regeneration, with a disused 19th-century railway viaduct and dilapidated wine warehouse district brought back to life and now thriving.

Bastille

No trace of the prison stormed in 1789 remains on the circular **place de la Bastille**. Even the column in the centre commemorates a later revolution, that of 1830. The area was largely ignored, until architect Carlos Ott was commissioned to create a new opera house, the **Opéra Bastille** (guided tours, tel: 01 40 01 19 70, <www.operadeparis. fr>) as one of Mitterrand's *grands projets (see page 21)*. Cutting-edge artists and designers, notably fashion designer Jean-Paul Gaultier, moved into the area, and now, in streets such as rue de la Couronne, traditional shops alternate with galleries and cool restaurants. North of the Bastille is rue Oberkampf, where there's a concentration of hip bars and boutiques.

The Opéra Bastille

To the south of the Bastille, at 15–121 avenue Daumesnil, is the **Viaduct des Arts**. In the golden age of the railways, the Viaduc de Paris, built in 1859, supported a train line from Bastille to the Bois de Vincennes. However, as the railways declined in the 20th century, the viaduct fell into disrepair. It was saved from demolition and reopened in 1998, with attractive glass-fronted workshops and craft boutiques occupying its arches.

Eastern Paris

In **Bercy**, old stone-walled warehouses and cobbled streets have been given a new lease of life in the shape of Bercy Village, centred on cour St-Emilion, home to boutiques, restaurants and cafés. On the north side of the Parc de Bercy, La Maison du Cinéma *(see page 94)* opened in 2005 as the home of the Cinémathèque de Paris, a film museum, research centre, repertory cinema, restaurant and film archive.

Also northeast of the Bastille is **Belleville**, home to an attractive park with panoramic views of Paris.

Père Lachaise

The Cimetière du Père Lachaise (open daily Nov–Mar 8am–5.30pm, slightly longer hours on Sun and Apr–Oct, <www.pere-lachaise.com>) has seen an estimated 1,350,000 burials since its foundation in 1804. It even served as a battleground in 1871, when the Communards made a last stand here: the Mur des Fédérés in the southeast corner marks the place where many were executed by firing squad. Tombs of the famous include those of painter Ingres, dancer Isadora Duncan and the composers Rossini and Chopin. Writers such as La Fontaine, Molière, Balzac, Proust and Oscar Wilde – honoured with a fine monument by Jacob Epstein – are also buried here. More recent arrivals include singers Edith Piaf and Jim Morrison, and actor Yves Montand.

CHAMPS-ELYSÉES, TROCADÉRO & WEST

The Champs-Elysées were designed by landscape architect André Le Nôtre in 1667 as an extension of the Tuileries *(see page 39)*. Initially the promenade only reached as far as the Rond-Point des Champs-Elysées (ie less than half its current length). Over a hundred years passed before the rest of the avenue, stretching up to the Arc de Triomphe, was completed. Its reputation has ebbed and flowed with the centuries, and it is currently experiencing something of a comeback as one of this city's most prestigious shopping strips.

Bird's-eye view of the Champs-Elysées

Champs-Elysées

The commercial stretch of the **Champs-Elysées** runs from the Rond-Point to the Arc de Triomphe. The landmark stores are the Virgin Megastore at Nos 52–60, where you can sample CDs until midnight; Guerlain at No. 68, with its Rococo-style façade and sumptuous interior; the Aladdin's cave of beauty products, Sephora, at No. 70; and Louis Vuitton at No. 101. The majority of the designer shops are concentrated around avenue Montaigne, the southern end of avenue George V and rue du Faubourg St-Honoré. This is fashion land, where prices for the majority are prohibitive, but window shopping is free. Fashionable bars and restaurants have mushroomed in the surrounding streets with new places including Senso, Tanjia, Spoon and Market.

On the southern side of the Champs, between place Clemenceau and the river, is the imposing, glass-domed **Grand Palais** (open Wed–Mon 10am–1pm to visitors with advance tickets and 1–8pm to those without reservations, ticket desks shut 30 mins before closing, <www.rmn.fr>), constructed for the 1900 World Fair. The Grand Palais hosts several major art exhibitions every year. It shares its colossal building with the **Palais de la Découverte** (open Tues–Sat 9.30am–6pm, Sun and bank hols 10am–7pm, <www.palais-decouverte.fr>) and includes among its displays a hands-on exhibition of the sciences, with a planetarium as centrepiece.

Across avenue Winston Churchill is the **Petit Palais** (open Tues 10am–8pm, Wed–Sun 10am–6pm), which houses the fine-art collection of the Musée des Beaux-Arts de la Ville de Paris.

Arc de Triomphe

Officially renamed **place Charles de Gaulle** after the death of the president in 1969, the circular area at the top of the Champs-Elysées is popularly known to Parisians as *l'Etoile* (the star), after the 12 avenues branching out from its centre. It is dominated by one of the most familiar Paris icons, the **Arc de Triomphe** (open daily 10am–10.30pm, Apr–Oct until 11pm, <www.monuments-nationaux.fr>). The arch is

Famous macaroons

Renowned in Paris for generations for its delectable macaroons, Ladurée, a bakery/restaurant at 75 avenue des Champs-Elysées, is always busy and very chic. Don't leave without trying the melt-in-the-mouth macaroons, which come in a multitude of flavours. There's also a branch at 16 rue Royale.

50m (164ft) high and 45m (148ft) wide. A trip to the top by the stairs (lift for the disabled only) affords excellent views. It is from here that you can best appreciate the *tour de force* of geometric planning that the avenues represent.

Napoleon I conceived of the Arc de Triomphe as a tribute to his armies, and it bears the names of hundreds of his marshals and generals, and dozens of victories. No defeats are recorded, naturally, although a few of the victories are debatable. Napoleon himself only ever saw a wood-and-canvas model, since the arch was not completed until the 1830s. It rapidly became the focus for state occasions, such as the return of the emperor's remains from St Helena in 1840 and the funeral of Victor Hugo in 1885. When Adolf Hitler arrived in Paris as conqueror in 1940, the Arc de Triomphe was the first sight he wanted to see. And at the Liberation, this was the spot where General de Gaulle commenced his triumphal march down the Champs-Elysées.

Arc de Triomphe

Under the arch is the grave of the Unknown Soldier, since 1920 the last resting place of a soldier who died in World War I. The eternal flame was lit here in 1923.

Trocadéro

Dominating place du Trocadéro is the **Palais de Chaillot**, built for the Paris World Fair of 1937. The imposing Art Deco palace was designed in the shape of an amphitheatre, with its wings following the original outline of the old Trocadéro in graceful symmetry.

The Art Deco Palais de Chaillot

The west wing is home to the **Musée de la Marine** (open Wed–Mon 10am–6pm, <www.musee-marine.fr>), which traces the history of the French navy. The east wing houses the **Cité de l'Architecture et du Patrimoine** (<www.archi.fr>), opened in 2007, combining Paris's old architecture museum with the Institut Français d'Architecture. Both a museum and a professional research centre, it hosts large-scale exhibitions and has a state-of-the-art public audio-visual centre.

On avenue des Nations-Unies is **Cinéaqua** (open daily 10am–8pm, <www.cineaqua.com>), a vast aquarium with cinema, animation studio – and sushi restaurant. 43 tanks contain 10,000 fish, grouped in mini marine ecosystems.

Down avenue du Président Wilson is the vast **Palais de Tokyo**, built as the Electricity Pavilion for the 1937 World Fair. One wing was intended to hold post-1905 fine art from the municipal fine-art collection; the other wing (now the Site de Création Contemporaine) was planned for the national collection of modern art, divided at that time between the Musée du Luxembourg and the Jeu de Paume. The **Musée d'Art Moderne de la Ville de Paris** (open Tues–Sun 10am–6pm) opened there in 1961. In 1977 the core collection of French and international art was given a new home at the Centre Pompidou *(see page 46)*. While the emphasis at the Pompidou is on international art, here the focus is on artists who worked in Paris.

In the other wing is the **Site de Création Contemporaine** (open Tues–Sun noon–12am, <www.palaisdetokyo.com>), where a multi-disciplinary programme focuses on young artists through exhibitions, performances and workshops.

Western Paris

West of the Palais de Chaillot, villagey Passy is an upmarket residential area with a couple of busy shopping streets (rue de Passy and rue de l'Assomption). However, it is also home to the atmospheric **Maison de Balzac** (47 rue Raynouard, open Tues–Sun 10am–6pm), where the writer penned much of his great opus *La Comédie Humaine*. The house remains furnished as it would have been at the time, with a rich collection of Balzacian manuscripts and memorabilia on show.

Also in the west of Paris is the **Musée Marmottan-Monet** (2 rue Louis-Boilly, open Tues–Sun 10am–6pm, <www.

Monet's *Impression, Soleil Levant* (c.1873)

marmottan.com>), showcase for the art assembled by collector Louis Marmottan (1856–1932). The displays are comprised mostly of Impressionist masterpieces, including works by Monet, Renoir, Manet and Gauguin, but there is also some exceptional First Empire furniture.

The **Musée Nissim de Camondo** (63 rue de Monceau, open Wed–Sun 10am–5pm), overlooking Parc Monceau, was built by a wealthy Jewish banking family in the style of the Petit Trianon *(see page 85)* at Versailles. The remarkable collection of tapestries, carpets, porcelain, furniture and paintings, all dating from the 18th century, were bequeathed to the state in 1935 by the passionate art collector, Count Moïse de Camondo, in memory of his son, Nissim, killed in action in 1917. The building and family history are as fascinating as the collection.

Also beside Parc Monceau is the **Musée Cernuschi** (7 avenue Vélasquez, open Tues–Sun 10am–5.45pm), one of the most important collections of Oriental art in Europe. The 19th-century financier Henri Cernuschi amassed the collection on a tour of China and Japan from 1871 to 1873, and built this mansion to house it.

Bois de Boulogne

In western Paris is the capital's biggest park, comprising 900 hectares (2,200 acres) of grassland, lakes and woods. There are bikes for rent outside its entrance for exploring. Napoleon III commissioned Baron Haussmann to transform a remnant of an old hunting forest along the lines of a London park, and the **Bagatelle**, once a royal retreat, is still the site of a lovely English garden. Also within the park is a craft museum, a boating lake, the **Jardin d'Acclimatation** (an amusement park with attractions for children) and two racecourses: Longchamp for flat races; Auteuil for steeplechases. Note, however, that in spite of police patrols, parts of the park after nightfall are considered to be among the most dangerous places in Paris.

MONTMARTRE & PIGALLE

With narrow, winding streets and dead-ends **Montmartre** ('*la Butte*', or the hill, to its residents) still has something of the hilltop village. For over 200 years it has been associated with artists and bohemians. The tourist *Montmartrobus* spares you the walk and shows you some of the area in a single tour, but the best way to discover Montmartre at your own pace is to start early, at the top. Take the Métro to Abbesses and the lift to the street (the stairs here seem endless) – and note the handsome Art Nouveau entrance as you leave. Rue Yvonne le Tac leads to the base station of a funicular railway.

Sacré-Coeur

The Sacré-Cœur

The funicular (Métro/bus tickets are valid) climbs to the terrace right in front of the Byzantine-style basilica of **Sacré-Cœur** (basilica open daily 6am–10.30pm, crypt and dome 10am–5.45pm). Standing at the highest point in Paris, it is one of the city's principal landmarks, and one of the few to remain controversial. Some parties still scorn it as a vulgar pastiche, and the working-class residents of the area resented it being erected as a symbol of penitence for the insurrection of the 1871 Commune (see page 19) – they did not feel in the least penitent. The Sacré-

Cœur's whiteness comes from the local Château-Landon limestone, which bleaches on contact with carbon dioxide in the air and hardens with age. For many, the best reason for visiting the basilica is the view of the city from the dome or the terrace below.

Last vineyard

At the corner of rue St-Vincent and rue des Saules, look out for the city's last surviving vineyard, the tiny Clos de Montmartre, which produces a wine that reputedly 'makes you jump like a goat'.

Place du Tertre

A few steps west of Sacré-Cœur is **St-Pierre-de-Montmartre**, one of the city's oldest churches. Consecrated in 1147, it is a significant work of early Gothic style, belied by its 18th-century façade. Nearby **place du Tertre** was once the centre of village life. The square is best visited during the early morning, before the pushy portrait artists set up their easels and the crowds of tourists take over.

In place Emile Goudeau, just downhill but artistically on an altogether much higher level, No. 13 was the site of the studio known as the **Bateau-Lavoir** (so-called because the building resembled the Seine's laundry boats, before it was destroyed by fire). It was here that Picasso, Georges Braque and Juan Gris developed Cubism, Modigliani painted, and Apollinaire wrote his first Surrealist verses. Some of their predecessors – Renoir, Van Gogh and Gauguin – once lived and worked just north of place du Tertre.

The **Cimetière de Montmartre** (open daily Nov–Mar 8.30am–5.30pm, slightly longer hours Sun and Apr–Oct) is at 20 avenue Rachel. The cemetery's more illustrious 'residents' include 19th-century society beauty Madame Récamier, composers Berlioz and Offenbach, the sculptor Degas, German poet Heinrich Heine and film director François Truffaut.

Pigalle

At the far end of rue Lepic, a market street renowned for its food shops and the site of several appealingly bohemian cafés, is place Blanche, where the ambience changes. On the corner of boulevard de Clichy is the iconic **Moulin Rouge**, still staging its nightly cabarets, although mostly to tourists. Next door is **La Loco**, a huge disco, pumping with the sounds of house, dance music and mainstream pop. Less artistic attractions abound in **Pigalle**, a powerhouse of the Paris sex trade for decades. Tassled curtains provide glimpses of smoky interiors, garish signs promote live sex shows and aggressive bouncers attempt to persuade tourists into 'naked extravaganzas'. However, Pigalle is changing from sleaze centre to hip night-spot. The cabarets which formerly occupied half the houses along rue des Martyrs are increasingly being taken over by hip clubs and trendy bars.

Moulin Rouge

LA VILLETTE

In northeast Paris, right against the Périphérique ring road, is **Parc de la Villette** (Métro: Porte de Pantin or Porte de la Villette, open daily 6am–1am, <www.villette.com>). Built on the site of an enormous abattoir, which was rendered obsolete by improved refrigeration techniques and poor design

The Géode

(the cows could not even get up the steps), 55 hectares (136 acres) of futuristic gardens surround a colossal science museum, the **Cité des Sciences et de l'Industrie** (open Tues–Sat 10am–6pm, Sun until 7pm, <www.cite-sciences.fr>). It is not a museum for academics: the exhibits are interactive, with buttons, keyboards and screens to keep mind and body alert.

Begin at 'L'Univers' (Universe), which has a spectacular planetarium and also provides explanation of the inexplicable Big Bang. 'La Vie' (Life) is an eclectic mix of medicine, agriculture and economics. 'La Matière' (Matter) reproduces a nuclear explosion and gives you the chance to land an Airbus 320, and 'La Communication' has displays of artificial intelligence, three-dimensional graphics and virtual reality.

La Géode (open Mon–Fri 10.30am–6.30pm, Sat until 9.30pm, Sun until 8.30pm, reservations advised during school holidays and on weekend afternoons, tel: 08 92 68 45 40, lines open noon–8pm, <www.lageode.fr>) is a giant silver ball housing a wraparound IMAX cinema; see the website for details of the programme. Also here are L'Argonaute, a retired naval submarine, and Cinaxe, a flight-simulator-cum-cinema that's definitely not for the queasy.

The former cattle market now houses a cultural and conference centre in the immense 19th-century Grande Halle, which reopened in 2007 after restoration. Next door, the **Cité de la Musique** is an edifice of angles designed by architect Christian de Portzamparc, and includes the **Musée de la Musique** (open Tues–Sat noon–6pm, Sun 10am–6pm, ticket desks close 45 mins prior to last entry, <www.cite-musique.fr>). Portzamparc also designed the national music and dance conservatory on the other side of the Grande Halle. The museum charts the development of classical, jazz and folk music and houses an impressive collection of over 4,500 musical instruments.

The gardens of the park are the biggest to be built in Paris since Haussmann's time. Designed by Bernard Tschumi and opened in 1993, they comprise several thematic areas such as the Jardin des Frayeurs Enfantines (Garden of Childhood Fears) with a huge dragon slide, and the Jardin des Vents (Garden of Winds), home to multicoloured bamboo. Abstraction continues in the form of Tschumi's folies: red angular 'tree houses' (minus the trees), each with a special function such as play area, workshop, daycare centre or café.

Along the Canal

The Paris canals were dug in 1821 as a transport link for the factories and warehouses in the area northeast of the Bastille. Shielded by trees, the canal is a popular strolling ground, particularly on balmy summer evenings. A pleasant way to experience it is by canal boat, starting either at Bastille or at La Villette. Sights en route include, at the bend in the canal, the trendy Chez Prune café and a row of pastel-coloured Antoine et Lili shopfronts, and on the opposite bank, the Hôtel du Nord, of French movie fame. Canal tours lasting around two and a half hours are run by Canauxrama. Tel: 01 42 39 15 00 or visit <www.canauxrama.com> for further details.

St-Germain-des-Prés, the heart of the Left Bank

LATIN QUARTER & ST-GERMAIN-DES-PRÉS

The area referred to as the Latin Quarter lies to the east of boulevard St-Michel. This maze of ancient streets and squares has been the stamping ground of students for nearly eight centuries, and Latin was virtually the mother tongue until Napoleon put a stop to it after the Revolution. West of boulevard St-Michel is St-Germain-des-Prés, the historic centre of literary Paris and existentialism, with the oldest church in Paris at its heart. Although these two areas have changed over the past few decades, with high fashion increasingly replacing high art, they still maintain their charm in tree-lined boulevards, narrow streets and manicured parks.

The Latin Quarter

Begin your visit to the Latin Quarter at **place St-Michel**, where students buy their books or gather around the grand

Books are big business

1860s fountain by Gabriel Davioud. From here, plunge into the narrow streets of the **St-Séverin** quarter to the east (rues St-Séverin, de la Harpe and Galande). Here, you'll find medieval streets busy with smoky Greek grills, Tunisian bakeries selling sticky date pastries, and art-house cinemas.

The early Gothic church of **St-Julien-le-Pauvre**, on the street of the same name, hosts recitals of chamber and religious music. Just across rue St-Jacques stands the exquisite 13th- to 15th-century flamboyant Gothic church of **St-Séverin**, in which Dante is said to have prayed and Saint-Saëns asked to be made honorary organist.

The Sorbonne

Named after the 13th-century college established by Robert de Sorbon for poor theological students, the university was later taken in hand by Cardinal Richelieu, who financed its reconstruction (1624–42). Few of the somewhat forbidding buildings are open to the public, but you can go inside the 17th-century **courtyard** with its ornate sundial and see the outside of the baroque library and domed church.

Protest against overcrowding, antiquated teaching, bureaucracy and the basis of the social system made the Sorbonne a focal point for unrest in 1968, a year of ferment across Europe. Over on the tree-shaded **place de la Sorbonne**, it's hard to imagine the police invading such a peaceful sanctuary – one that for centuries guaranteed student immunity. But invade they did, and revolt exploded onto the streets. Students and workers made common cause, and there followed widespread national strikes that threatened the survival of the government. In the aftermath of the revolts, the Sorbonne was absorbed into the huge Paris Universities monolith and lost its independence.

Musée National du Moyen Age – Musée de Cluny

Opposite the Sorbonne's rue des Ecoles entrance is the **Musée National du Moyen Age** (6 place Paul-Painlevé, open Wed–Mon 9.15am–5.45pm, <www.musee-moyenage.fr>), still often called by its former name, the Musée de Cluny. Once the residence of the Abbots of Cluny, the museum houses one of the world's finest collections of medieval artefacts.

Its star attraction is the exquisite, 15th-century tapestry *La Dame à la Licorne* (The Lady and the Unicorn), six pieces depicting the five senses and the temptations that the eponymous lady vows to overcome. The museum also holds 21 of the original heads of the Kings of Judah, sculpted in 1220 for Notre-Dame cathedral but vandalised in the Revolution.

Musée National du Moyen Age

The Hôtel de Cluny was built on the remains of a huge Gallo-Roman bath house believed to have been erected in AD200 by the guild of *nautes* (boatmen) – ships' prows are carved on the arch supports of the frigidarium (cold bath house).

Great thinkers

Among those interred in the Panthéon are novelist Emile Zola, socialist Jean Jaurès, Louis Braille and Pierre and Marie Curie (the latter was the first woman buried here).

Panthéon

Designed for Louis XV in 1755 as the church of Ste-Geneviève (patron saint of Paris), the neoclassical **Panthéon** (open daily during summer 9.30am–6.30pm, during winter 10am–6.15pm) was secularised in the Revolution to serve as a mausoleum. For most of the 19th century its status oscillated between secular and sacred, but Victor Hugo's funeral in 1885 settled the issue in favour of a secular mausoleum. The interior is sparse, with its walls covered by 19th-century murals by Puvis de Chavannes. The crypt is a maze of corridors lined with cells containing tombs.

Rue Mouffetard

The old streets behind the Panthéon, where the bustling **rue Mouffetard** and its offshoots meet are a village within the city. The stalls of rue Mouffetard's morning market are piled with appetising produce. Here, and in tiny **place de la Contrescarpe** nearby, you will find a large choice of ethnic restaurants. A little to the east, signs to **Arènes de Lutèce** point to a little park that is the site of a Roman amphitheatre, partially restored after its remains were found in the 19th century.

In rue St-Etienne-du-Mont is the church of **St-Etienne-du-Mont** (open Tues–Sun 10am–7pm). This was the parish church of the Abbey of Ste-Geneviève and still houses a shrine to the city's patron saint. The real highlight is the Renaissance rood screen (1541), the only one in Paris.

Institut du Monde Arabe

Back by the Seine, but heading east, stroll past the university complex that stands on the site of the former Halles aux Vins (wine market). Designed by architect Jean Nouvel, the nearby **Institut du Monde Arabe** (1 rue des Fossés-St-Bernard, open Tues–Sun 10am–6pm, <www.imarabe.org>) was built with the help of 16 Arab nations to foster cultural links between Europe and the Islamic world. Inside, a museum traces the cultures of the Arab world with first-rate exhibits. A library of over 40,000 volumes covers all aspects of Arab culture. There are fine views from the rooftop restaurant.

Institut du Monde Arabe

Jardin des Plantes

Adjacent is the **Jardin des Plantes** (open daily 8am–7.30pm in summer, 8am–5.30pm in winter), created by Louis XIII as 'a royal garden of medicinal plants' and still a fine botanical and decorative garden, with exotic plants in the hot-houses. The oldest tree in Paris is located here.

The adjoining **Muséum National d'Histoire Naturelle** (open Wed–Mon 10am–6pm) has renovated its venerable exhibits of fossils, skeletons, butterflies and mineral samples. The **Grande Galerie de l'Evolution** (36 rue Geoffroy-St-Hilaire, opening times as above, until 8pm Sat in summer) devoted to the origins of all life on earth, is outstanding.

St-Germain-des-Prés

The historical heart of literary Paris, **St-Germain-des-Prés** covers an area stretching roughly from St-Sulpice to the Seine and bounded to the west by boulevard St-Germain. Its elegant streets house chic boutiques, yet it still retains a sense of animation, with crowded cafés spilling out on to the pavements. In the 1950s the area became a breeding ground for literature and philosophy. Existentialists, led by Jean-Paul Sartre, Simone de Beauvoir and Albert Camus, gathered in cafés such as **Les Deux Magots** and **Café Flore**.

Boulevard St-Germain

That said, the days of black polo-necks and beret-clad existentialists engaged in heated literary debate are over. The area has now been colonised by designers and upmarket antiques dealers. The Marché St-Germain shows just how much it has changed. After a tasteful restoration, the old market hall now contains fashion boutiques, a swimming pool, an auditorium and small food market.

On the opposite side of the boulevard, the church of **St-Germain-des-Prés** (open Mon–Sat 8am–7.45pm, Sun 9am–8pm) is the oldest in Paris, parts of it dating from the 11th century. It is named after a former cardinal of Paris, who is buried here.

Académie Française

The august Palais de l'Institut de France, home of the **Académie Française**, is north of the church of St-Germain, on quai de Conti by the Pont des Arts. It was designed by Louis le Vau in 1668 to harmonise with the Louvre across the river. The Institut began as a school for the sons of provincial gentry, financed by a legacy of Cardinal Mazarin. Then, in 1805, the building was turned over to the Institut, which comprises the Académie Française, supreme arbiter of the French language founded by Cardinal Richelieu in 1635, and the Académies des Belles-Lettres, Sciences, Beaux-Arts, and Sciences Morales et Politiques.

New Left Bank

The 'new' Rive Gauche (Left Bank) is the biggest urban renewal project since the mid-1850s, when Baron Haussmann razed the city's medieval heart to carve out stately, tree-lined boulevards. Newly created streets and buildings are going up in a zone of rusty factories and disused railway tracks that extend south along the river from the Gare d'Austerlitz. The area's centrepiece is the **Bibliothèque Nationale de France François Mitterrand** (open Mon 2–7pm, Tues–Sat 9am–7pm, Sun 1–7pm, <www.bnf.fr>). Designed by Dominique Perrault and opened in 1996, the library cost over US$1 billion and is more expensive to maintain than the Louvre. Its 90-m (300-ft) high glass towers evoke open books.

Musée Delacroix and St-Sulpice

Tucked away in a tiny square a short walk from the church of St-Germain-des-Prés is the delightful **Musée Eugène Delacroix** (6 place Furstenberg, open Wed–Mon 9.30am–4.30pm, <www.musee-delacroix.fr>). The painter lived here from 1857 to 1863 while he was working on frescoes in a chapel at St-Sulpice. Temporary exhibitions are held in the airy former studio, while letters and personal effects are displayed in the house. There's also a wonderfully calm garden out back.

It's just a short hop south across boulevard St-Germain-des-Prés to place St-Sulpice, the eastern side of which is dominated by Jean-Baptiste Servandoni's Italianesque church of the same name. **St-Sulpice** (daily 7.30am–7.30pm) is notable for its vast towers (under restoration), one of which is higher than the other, and for painter Eugène Delacroix's massive oil-and-wax frescoes, completed two years before his death.

Leisurely pursuits in the Jardin du Luxembourg

Jardin du Luxembourg

The beautifully landscaped **Jardin du Luxembourg** is the quintessential Paris park. Students read, relax or play tennis, old men meet under the chestnut trees to play chess or a game of *boules*, lovers huddle together on metal chairs, and children sail boats across the carp-filled pond and ride a merry-go-round designed by Charles Garnier, architect of the historic opera house *(see page 43)*. At the northern end of the gardens, the Italianate **Palais du Luxembourg** (guided tours by appointment, tel: 01 44 54 19 49 for individuals, <www.senat.fr>), built for Marie de Médicis in the early 17th century, now houses the French Senate. The adjacent Petit Luxembourg is the official home of the president of the Senate.

The **Musée National du Luxembourg** (19 rue de Vaugirard, open Mon, Fri, Sat 11am–10pm, Tues, Thur 11am–7pm, Sun 9am–7pm, <www.museeduluxembourg.fr>) hosts art exhibitions.

Odéon

The Odéon district lies between the Latin Quarter and St-Germain-des-Prés. Across boulevard St-Germain, at the Carrefour de l'Odéon, a statue of the Revolutionary leader Georges Danton marks the spot where his old house once stood. Fellow Revolutionary Camille Desmoulins lived at No. 2 before storming the Bastille in 1789. Others plotted to the north in neighbouring streets that now shelter some of the most expensive boutiques and apartments in Paris.

From here, rue de l'Odéon, the first street in Paris to have gutters and pavements, leads to place de l'Odéon. The neoclassical Odéon Théâtre de l'Europe (tel: 01 44 85 40 40, <www.theatre-odeon.fr>), founded in 1782, is home to one of France's leading state theatre companies. It puts on a repertoire of mainly foreign playwrights (Büchner, Chekhov, Shakespeare, etc), sometimes in original-language productions.

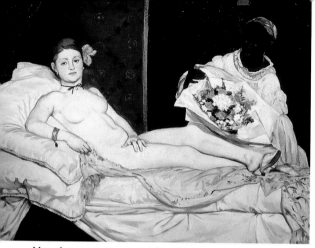

Manet's once-controversial *Olympia*

AROUND THE EIFFEL TOWER

When the Paris nobility moved out of the Marais *(see page 48)* in the 18th century, and Versailles tumbled, the rich and famous built new town houses across the river from the Tuileries, in the 7th *arrondissement*. Not only is this chic district rich with upmarket architecture, it is also has a wealth of visitor attractions, with highlights including the Musée d'Orsay, the Eiffel Tower, the Invalides and the Musée Rodin.

Musée d'Orsay
'The station is superb and truly looks like a Fine Arts Museum, and since the Fine Arts Museum resembles a station, I suggest… we make the change while we still can,' said painter Edouard Detaille in 1900. In 1986, his joke became a reality. Linked to the Tuileries by the Passerelle Solférino footbridge, the converted 19th-century hotel-cum-railway station was trans-

formed into the **Musée d'Orsay** (open Tues–Sun 9.30am–6pm, until 9.45pm in June, <www.musee-orsay.fr>), devoted to French art from 1848 to 1914. Keeping the exterior much as it was, Italian architect Gae Aulenti adapted the interior to house many of the previously scattered works of that period, including the superb Impressionist collection formerly held in the Jeu de Paume *(see page 40)*. Sculpture is well represented, and photography is covered from its inception (1839) onwards.

Many visitors start at the top with the Impressionists and Post-Impressionists: Renoir, Cézanne, Manet, Monet, Toulouse-Lautrec, Degas and Van Gogh (this is the best collection of his work outside Amsterdam, with several works from the frenzied months of activity before he died in 1890). Outstanding in the ground-floor collections are the vast canvases of Gustave Courbet. There is a café high up behind the huge old station clock, and on the middle level the station hotel's beautifully restored restaurant is back in use.

Assemblée Nationale

Geographically if not temperamentally part of the Left Bank, the Palais Bourbon is the seat of the **Assemblée Nationale** (33 bis quai d'Orsay), the Lower House of the French Parliament. Built from 1722 to 1728 for Louis XIV's daughter the Duchess of Bourbon, in the style of the Grand Trianon at Versailles, it forms a fittingly stately riverside façade for the grand 7th *arrondissement*. Napoleon added the Grecian columns facing the Pont de la Concorde, but the palace

Sculpture at the Palais Bourbon

is more graceful when seen from its entrance on the south side. Access is available only on written request or invitation by a deputy. A privileged few are allowed to see the Delacroix paintings, illustrating the history of civilisation, in the library.

Musée Rodin

The Prime Minister's residence, Hôtel Matignon (57 rue de Varenne), is a short walk from the Assemblée Nationale. Its private park has a music pavilion favoured for secret strategy sessions. On the same elegant street, at No. 77, Rodin's former mansion, the delightful 18th-century Hôtel Biron, is now a showcase for the sculptor's works in the form of the

Rodin's *The Thinker*

Musée National Rodin (open Tues–Sun, Apr–Sept museum 9.30am–5.45pm, park until 6.45pm, last admission at 5.15pm, Oct–Mar museum 9.30am–4.45pm, park until 5pm, last admission at 4.15pm, <www.musee-rodin.fr>). Many of the most famous sculptures are in the gardens. Highlights include *The Kiss* (removed from the Chicago World Fair of 1893 for being too shocking), *The Thinker* (reputedly Dante contemplating the Inferno), *The Burghers of Calais* and *Balzac*, depicting the writer as a mountain of a man. Also on display are works by Camille Claudel, the most famous of Rodin's mistresses.

Les Invalides

One of the most important sights in this area is the monumental **Hôtel des Invalides** (open Oct–Mar daily 10am–5pm, until 6pm Apr–Sept, <www.invalides.org>), established by Louis XIV as the first national hospital and retirement home for soldiers wounded in action. At one time it housed approximately 6,000 veterans, but Napoleon Bonaparte commandeered a large part of the building for the **Musée de l'Armée** (opening times as above).

Gilded dome of the Invalides

The Invalides came to symbolise the glory of Napoleon himself, when his remains were brought back from St Helena in 1840 for burial in the chapel under the golden **Dôme** (opening times as above, until 7pm 15 June–15 Sept). The emperor's son, who died of tuberculosis in Vienna, is buried in the crypt; his remains were sent here by Hitler in 1940.

The main courtyard allows access to the adjoining church of **St-Louis-des-Invalides**, decorated with flags taken by French armies in battle. The courtyard itself contains the 18 cannons, including eight taken from Vienna, that Napoleon ordered to be fired on great occasions, including the birth of his son in 1811. The cannons sounded again for the 1918 Armistice and the funeral of Marshal Foch in 1929.

Southwest of the Invalides is the **Ecole Militaire**, where officers have trained since the middle of the 18th century. Their former parade ground, the vast **Champ de Mars**, is

La Pagode

The area around Les Invalides is well worth exploring: start with Paris's quirkiest cinema and tea house, La Pagode in rue de Babylone. The tea is strong, the gardens tropical, and the films right up-to-date.

now a green park stretching all the way to the Eiffel Tower. This was the site of horse races in the 1780s and of five World Fairs between 1867 and 1937. In the 20th century, the Champs became the front lawn of the Left Bank's most luxurious residences.

The Eiffel Tower

For most people the ultimate Paris monument is still the **Tour Eiffel**, or Eiffel Tower (open daily Sept–mid-Jun 9.30am–11.45pm, with last lift 11pm, or 10.30pm for top floor, steps 9.30am–6.30pm; mid-Jun–Aug 9am–12.45am, with last lift midnight, or 11pm for top floor, steps 9.30am–12.45am, tel: 01 44 11 23 23, <www.tour-eiffel.fr>). When Gustave Eiffel's icon of iron girders was chosen as the centrepiece to the World Fair of 1889, he claimed enthusiastically, 'France will be the only country with a 300-m flagpole!' But his designs were met with a barrage of opposition. The architect of the opera house Charles Garnier and the novelist Guy de Maupassant were its most vocal opponents; Maupassant organised a protest picnic under the tower's four legs – 'the only place out of sight of the wretched construction'.

However, the Paris public loved their new tower, and only a few years later it was being lauded by writers and artists such as Apollinaire, Jean Cocteau, Raoul Dufy and Maurice Utrillo. At 321m (1,054ft) the tower was the world's tallest building until 1931, when New York's Empire State Building was constructed. Surviving a proposal for its demolition in 1909, when the placing of a radio transmitter at the top gave it a valuable practical function, the tower is now climbed by some six million visitors a year.

There are 360 steps to the first level, where there is an audio-visual presentation on the tower's history, and another 700 to the second; both of these floors are also accessible by lifts – there is always a queue for these, which travel 100,000km (62,137 miles) a year. On the third level (accessible by lift only) is a glassed-in viewing platform and Gustave Eiffel's sitting room. On a clear day panoramas of over 65km (40 miles) can be enjoyed. There are two restaurants, including the Michelin-starred Jules Verne *(see page 142)* on the second floor. On hot days the ironwork expands, enabling the tower to grow as much as 15cm (6in). Even in the strongest of winds, it has never swayed more than 12cm (4in). Up to 40 tonnes of paint have to be used when it is painted every seven years.

The Eiffel Tower

Tribal art inside the Musée du Quai Branly

Musée du Quai Branly

Just northeast of the tower, at 37 quai Branly, is Jacques Chirac's cultural legacy, the **Musée du Quai Branly** (open Tues–Sun 10am–6.30pm, Thur until 9.30pm, <www.quai branly.fr>), opened in 2006. The museum houses a collection of around 300,000 objects of art from Africa, Asia, the Americas and Oceania, with over 3,600 items actually on display. With its colonial overtones, the collection has sparked some controversy, but the building itself – a striking foliage-covered scarlet edifice designed by architect Jean Nouvel – has been more warmly received.

MONTPARNASSE

Named after the mountain home of the classical Muses, Paris's 'Mount Parnassus' was a mound left after quarrying. In the 1920s, the quarter took over from Montmartre as the stamping ground of the city's artistic colony, led by Picasso. American expatriates such as Ernest Hemingway, Gertrude Stein, F. Scott Fitzgerald and John Dos Passos liked the free-living atmosphere and added to the mystique themselves.

One of Henry Miller's hang-outs, Le Select (99 boulevard du Montparnasse) opened as an all-night bar in 1925. *Les Six*, the group of composers that included Milhaud, Poulenc and Honegger, met here. La Coupole *(see page 142)*, opposite at No. 102, was a favourite with Sartre and de Beauvoir in the years after World War II; it has been rebuilt and now seats 400 people. Le Dôme at No. 108 has lost some of its character since the days of Modigliani and Stravinsky, with elaborate remodelling. Across the street, at No. 105, Picasso, Derain and Vlaminck used to meet at La Rotonde. At the junction of boulevard du Montparnasse and boulevard St-Michel, La Closerie des Lilas is where Lenin and Trotsky dreamt of a Russian Revolution, and where Hemingway and his friends met after World War I.

Today the attraction isn't immediately evident: boulevard du Montparnasse is plain by Paris standards, and most of the haunts where the 'Lost Generation' found itself have been polished and painted, or even entirely rebuilt. But people still pay elevated prices for the privilege of sitting in a seat that may have been warmed by Modigliani, Lenin or Sartre.

The 59-storey, 210-m (689-ft) **Tour Montparnasse** (33 avenue du Maine, open daily in summer 9.30am–11.30pm,

City catacombs

Beneath Montparnasse are the city's catacombs (entrance on place Denfert-Rochereau, open Tues–Sun 10am–4.45pm), old quarries whose corridors were used for the reburial of millions of skeletons from over-crowded cemeteries and charnel houses. Unidentified, the bones are stacked on shelves and sometimes artfully arranged into macabre patterns.

in winter 9.30am–10.30pm, <www.tourmontparnasse56.com>) may be something of an egregious eyesore, but the view from the top is marvellous.

The **Cimetière du Montparnasse** (entrance on boulevard Edgar Quinet, open Mar–Nov 8.30am–5.45pm, Sat from 9am, slightly shorter hours in winter) contains the tombs of composers Saint-Saëns and César Franck, writer Maupassant and poet Baudelaire, plus Alfred Dreyfus, the Jewish army officer whose conviction on trumped-up spying charges split the nation. Also buried here are car maker André Citroën, Vichy prime minister Pierre Laval (executed while dying from a suicide attempt) and philosopher Jean-Paul Sartre and his writer companion Simone de Beauvoir.

LA DÉFENSE

Follow the long avenue de la Grande-Armée down from the Arc de Triomphe, and the battery of towers looms larger and larger beyond the elegant, leafy suburb of Neuilly. Cross the river and you are in a mini-Manhattan that has sprouted since 1969 to become a mini-city in its own right.

The **Grande Arche** (open daily Apr–Sept 10am–8pm, Oct–Mar 10am–7pm, <www.grandearche.com>) is further away than most of the towers, and only when you get close do you realise how big it is. A hollow cube 110m (360ft) high and 106m (347ft) wide, it could straddle the Champs-Elysées and tuck Notre-Dame underneath it. Built with re-markable speed (Danish architect Johann-Otto von Sprekelsen won the contest in 1983 and the arch was completed in time for the bicentennial of the French Revolution in 1989), the Grande Arche stands on an axis with the Arc de Triomphe and the Louvre. Its white gables are clothed in Carrara marble, the outer façades with a combination of grey marble and glass; the inside walls are covered with aluminium. The two 'legs' contain offices, while the roof houses conference rooms and exhibition spaces. A bubble lift whisks you up through a fibreglass and Teflon 'cloud', held by steel cables, but the ride to the top is expensive and the view not much more striking than the one from the terrace.

Increasing numbers of visitors and office-workers have given rise to a growing number of shops, cinemas, hotels and restaurants at La Défense. One of the biggest new arrivals is the 16-screen UGC Ciné Cité La Défense cinema complex.

Across the main concourse a 12-m (39-ft) bronze thumb by César literally sticks out like a sore thumb. Stroll down the tiers of terraces and you will discover even more statues, fountains and murals by Miró, Calder and other modern artists, all detailed on street-plans given out at information desks.

The Grande Arche at La Défense

Grand formality at Versailles

EXCURSIONS

Versailles

Louis XIV's palace at **Versailles** is as extravagant as the Sun King was himself. A visit to the château takes most or all of a day and entails a lot of walking. Versailles is 24km (15 miles) southwest of Paris, by road (N10); by train from Gare St-Lazare to Versailles; by RER (line C5) to Versailles-Rive Gauche; or by Métro to Pont de Sèvres, then bus 171. Palace: open Tues–Sun Apr–Oct 9am–6.30pm, Nov–Mar until 5.30pm. Marie Antoinette's Estate (incl. Petit Trianon): open daily Apr–Oct noon–7.30pm, Nov–Mar noon–6.30pm. Grand Trianon: open daily Apr–Oct noon–6.30pm, Nov–Mar noon–5.30pm. Gardens: open daily Apr–Oct 9am–sunset (except when the musical extravaganzas 'Grandes Eaux Musicales' are held, see website for details), Nov–Mar 9am–sunset; <www.chateauversailles.fr>.

Highlights of the interior include: the baroque **Royal Chapel**; the **State Apartments**, in which Louis XIV entertained; the Salon de Diane, where he played billiards; the 73-m (240-ft) long **Galerie des Glaces** (Hall of Mirrors); and the King's Bedroom, where Louis died of gangrene in 1715. In the Queen's Bedroom, 19 royal children were born, the births often attended by members of the court, as was the custom.

The grandest façade faces west to the gardens, where the fountains begin to play at 3.30pm on three Sundays a month (May–Sept). The **Grand Trianon**, the small palace Louis XIV used when he wanted to escape the vast château; the **Petit Trianon**, favoured by Louis XV; and the **Hameau** and miniature farm, where Louis XVI's queen, Marie-Antoinette, reputedly played at being a country girl, are also worth a visit.

Fontainebleau

The seat of sovereigns from Louis IX to Napoleon III and a glittering example of French Mannerism, the château at **Fontainebleau** (open Wed–Mon Jun–Sept 9.30am–6pm, Oct–May 9.30am–5pm, last admission 45 mins before closing, <www.musee-chateau-fontainebleau.fr>) makes a pleasant day trip from Paris. Here Louis XIV signed the Revocation of the Edict of Nantes in 1685, and Napoleon I signed his first act of abdication in 1814. More recently (1945–65) Fontainebleau was the headquarters of the military branch of NATO. Fontainebleau is 64km (40 miles) southeast of Paris by the A6 or by train from Gare de Lyon, then bus to the château.

The château at Fontainebleau

Malmaison

Set in lovely grounds, the château at **Malmaison** (open Apr–Sept Mon, Wed–Fri 10am–5.45pm, Sat, Sun 10am–6.15pm, Oct–Mar Mon, Wed–Fri 10am–12.30pm and 1.30–5.15pm, Sat, Sun 10am–12.30pm and 1.30–5.45pm, <www.chateau-malmaison.fr>) was the home of Napoleon's wife, Josephine, who continued to live here after their divorce. Many of her possessions are on display. Malmaison is 6km (4 miles) west of Paris. Métro: Grande Arche de La Défense, then bus 258, or RER to Rueil-Malmaison, followed by a walk or short taxi ride.

Vaux-le-Vicomte

This 17th-century château (open mid-Mar–mid-Nov Mon–Fri 10am–1pm and 2–6pm, Sat–Sun 10am–6pm, candlelit visits May–mid-Oct Sat 8pm–midnight, Fri also Jul–Aug, <www.vaux-le-vicomte.com>) was designed by Louis Le Vau, André Le Nôtre and Charles Le Brun for Louis XIV's finance minister, Fouquet. No sooner was it completed than the king had its owner arrested for embezzlement and jailed for life. Vaux-le-Vicomte is 55km (35 miles) southeast of Paris on the N5 or by train from Gare de Lyon to Melun, then a taxi ride.

Giverny

Claude Monet lived at this house in **Giverny** (open Apr–Oct Tues–Sun 9.30am–6pm, last admission 5.30pm, <www.fondation-monet.com>) from 1883 to 1926 and painted the gardens many times, especially the water lilies. Giverny is situated 85km (53 miles) northwest of Paris by the A13, D181 and D5, or by train from Gare St-Lazare to Vernon, with a shuttle bus from the station to Giverny.

Disneyland Resort Paris

Disney's ambitious recreation complex also encompasses hotels, restaurants, a convention centre, a golf course, tennis

Monet's *Bridge over a Pool of Water Lilies*

courts and several swimming pools – and attracts over 12 million visitors a year. In the theme park itself, Main Street USA, recapture the traditions of small-town America at the turn of the 20th century, leads to four other 'lands' – Frontierland, Adventureland, Fantasyland and Discoveryland. Each themed section has a variety of fun experiences to offer. Hosts Mickey and Minnie Mouse, Goofy, Donald Duck and Pluto wander around in their familiar costumes, posing with visitors. Every day at 3pm there's a parade including floats inspired by the famous Disney movies. In the **Walt Disney Studios Park** visitors can explore film sets and take part in scenes.

The resort is situated 32km (20 miles) east of Paris, near to Marne-la-Vallée. A motorway gives access from the city and the airports, Charles-de-Gaulle and Orly. Speedy commuter trains (RPEER line A) from the capital and even faster long-distance trains (TGV) serve Marne-la-Vallée/Chessy station near the entrance.

WHAT TO DO

Sightseeing in Paris is only part of the pleasure of a visit. Its shops, ranging from high-end boutiques and speciality stores to flea markets, are among the best in the world. The town also provides plenty of opportunities for fitness enthusiasts and fans of spectator sports. As for cultural entertainment, the city offers a wide variety of plays, films and music.

SHOPPING

How better to appreciate the city's beauty and character than to window-shop in elegant place Vendôme, meander along boulevard St-Germain, rummage through the book stalls on the banks of the Seine or peer into the eccentric dens of the covered passages? Paris has a wonderful variety of shops, and there is still a strong tradition of small specialist retailers.

What to Buy Where

Paris's different *quartiers* each have their own mood and atmosphere, and their shops often reflect their history and the type of people who live there. In terms of fashion, expect boho designers in hilly Montmartre; designer couture along avenue Montaigne and rue du Faubourg-St-Honoré; and cool, contemporary streetwear around Les Halles and rue Etienne-Marcel.

Other areas take a bit more delving into: the exclusive residential western sector of the 7th *arrondissement* is good for traditional menswear and equipment for the golfing

Gourmet paradise

Paris is a remarkably well-fed city, and every *quartier* has its chocolatiers, superb patisseries and boulangeries, delicatessens, ripe-smelling cheese shops and bustling street markets.

Department store Au Printemps

brigade, along with upmarket interior design boutiques and furnishing fabrics. Chic place Vendôme is the place in which to find sparkling, diamond-encrusted baubles, but you'll discover more original jewellery in St-Germain or the Marais. Similarly, whereas opulent 18th-century antiques are sold around quai Voltaire in the 7th and rue du Faubourg-St-Honoré in the 8th, retro furnishing and ceramics from the 1960s and 1970s are popular near the more alternative Bastille or Montmartre.

This said, the shopping map of Paris is far from static, reflecting an ebb and flow that goes with the rise and fall of different areas. The Champs-Elysées, which zigzagged from the epitome of glamour in the early 20th century to that of tourist dross in the 1980s, started returning to favour with a vengeance at the end of the 1990s. Long-staid rue St-Honoré is now the focus for a more avant-garde fashion set, chasing trends at concept store Colette. Equally in the past few years, designer fashion has migrated to once-literary St-

Germain, to the chagrin of those who bemoan the disappearance of favourite bookshops and foodstores.

Whereas the Marais was first fashionable in the early 17th century, it fell into decline with the departure of Louis XIV and his court to Versailles, and only began its slow recovery in the 1960s. But since the 1990s, restoration of its beautiful *hôtels particuliers* and the installation of several important museums have turned the area into a highly international district with many youthful fashion boutiques and quirky gift shops.

A parallel specialist enclave is the Marais's gay area, with its hub around the attractive rue Vieille-du-Temple. The past few years have seen the arrival of not just bars but gay-oriented bookshops and clothing stores, often replacing Jewish bookshops and bakeries in what had long been a Jewish district.

Other areas reflect the changing population of Paris. In the 13th *arrondissement,* in the 'Chinatown' quarter with its large South-East Asian population, you'll find Chinese supermarkets and *patisseries* among the high-rise tower blocks. Other previously overlooked territories have arrived on the retail map, notably along the Canal St-Martin, where women's fashion retailer Antoine et Lili set up three colourful, kitsch shops.

Galerie Vivienne

Other *quartiers* have not fared quite as well: Les Halles seems to be in perpetual decline, with its flagging array of unappealing, brash chain stores and dodgy reputation, and the aristocratic past of boulevards Bonne Nouvelle and Montmartre is a distant memory blurred by the ranks of discount stores and fast-food chains there.

Markets

Paris's markets pull in bargain hunters, gourmets and collectors alike. The fleamarkets of Paris range from the huge, classy Marché de St-Ouen to the tatty Marché de Montreuil and the venerable Marché d'Aligre. Another type of market is the 'roving' street market, held on two or three mornings a week (7am–2.30pm); at these you may find the most authentic produce and a true local flavour that varies from *quartier* to *quartier*.

In addition there are over 50 street markets; some have just a few stalls, while others, such as Marché Bastille or avenue Daumesnil, stretch for hundreds of metres and have superb ranges. Market streets, including rue Mouffetard, in the Latin Quarter, have food shops with stalls that spill on to the pavement and are open Tuesday to Saturday all day, with a long break for lunch, and on Sunday morning. For a full list with opening times, see 'Les marchés parisiens' at <www.paris.fr>.

Chic fashions on avenue Montaigne

SPORTS

The city caters fairly well for the sports enthusiast. You can find details on sporting events in the Wednesday edition of *Le Figaro*. For information (in French) on sporting facilities, contact Allô-Sports (tel: 08 20 00 75 75).

Spectator Sports

Football and rugby fans can watch games at the huge **Stade de France**, built for the 1998 World Cup. The stadium (rue Francis de Pressensé, St-Denis, tel: 01 55 93 00 00, <www.stade france.fr>, daily 10am–6pm, except when events are taking place) is also used for rock concerts, seating 100,000 spectators. The Parc des Princes in the 16th *arrondissement* is home to Paris's premier division football team, Paris St-Germain. The huge **Palais Omnisports Paris Bercy** (8 boulevard de Bercy, 75012, tel: 01 44 68 44 68, <www.bercy.fr>) hosts events including football, ice sports, motor sports and horse riding.

For racing, the Grand Prix de l'Arc de Triomphe takes place in October, at Longchamp in the Bois de Boulogne.

Participant Sports

The few public tennis courts in Paris, such as those at the Jardin du Luxembourg, are available on a first-come-first-served basis. Municipal swimming pools include the new Piscine Josephine Baker that floats on the Seine. For details of municipal sports facilities, see <www.sport. paris.fr>. The Bois de Boulogne, quais de Seine and Canal St-Martin offer good cycling opportunities; the Fédération Française de Cyclotourisme, tel: 01 44 16 88 88, has details of cycling clubs.

Sporting events

Major sporting events include the Six Nations Cup in Feb/March, the Marathon in April, and the French Tennis Open in May/June at the Stade Roland-Garros.

ENTERTAINMENT

For listings of what's on in Paris, buy one of the weekly guides, *Pariscope* or *L'Officiel des Spectacles*, both of which come out on Wednesday. *Figaroscope*, the Wednesday supplement of *Le Figaro* newspaper, is another good source of information. The tourist office also has up-to-date information (in several languages) on what's on. See also <www.paris-info.com>.

Theatre

The main national theatre is the **Comédie Française** (1 place Colette, 75001, tel: 01 44 58 15 15, <www.comedie-francaise. fr>, where work by such revered writers as Molière and Racine are performed. Modern classics are also shown here. Other key theatres include the Théâtre du Vieux Colombier (21 rue du Vieux-Colombier, 75006, <www.theatreduvieux colombier.com>, for small-scale productions of classical and modern drama, and the Théâtre du Châtelet (2 rue Edouard Colonne, 75001, <www.chatelet-theatre.com>, for opera,

Cinema

Paris has numerous multi-screen cinemas showing the latest block-busters, but if you'd rather see a French classic, there are a number of good art-house cinemas too. Most cinemas in the centre of Paris show films in their original language with sub-titles in French ('VO' – *version originale*), though once you get out of the city centre, mainstream films are usually dubbed ('VF' – *version française*). For a unique cinematic experience visit **La Pagode** (57bis rue de Babylone, 75007, tel: 01 45 55 48 48), where the latest films are shown in a tranquil Japanese setting complete with a tea room. Cinema buffs can also pay homage at the **Cinémathèque Française**, 51 rue de Bercy, 75012, <www. cinematheque francaise.com>, in a Cubist building by Frank Gehry.

classical concerts and the occasional ballet.

Music and Ballet

Both **opera** and **ballet** are staged in the lavish Palais Garnier (place de l'Opéra) and in the modern Opéra Bastille (2bis place de la Bastille). For details visit <www.operadeparis.fr>.

'Little sparrow', Edith Piaf

The French take their **jazz** seriously, and Paris has many clubs. An established venue is the Caveau de la Huchette (5 rue de la Huchette, <www.caveaudelahuchette>), which opens nightly at 9.30pm. Le Sunset/Sunside (60 rue des Lombards, <www.sunset-sunside.com> offers two jazz clubs in one: electric jazz and world music, plus acoustic. Bigger names perform at New Morning (rue des Petites-Ecuries) and the Lionel Hampton club at the Méridien Etoile (Porte Maillot).

Pop and rock concerts are held at the Zénith in the Parc de la Villette *(see page 63)*, Parc-des-Princes (Métro: Porte de St-Cloud) and the Palais Omnisports Paris Bercy *(see page 93)*. Ticket offices *(billeteries)* at branches of the FNAC books and records chain or Virgin Megastore on the Champs-Elysées will have details of what groups are in town.

Cabarets

Lavish floor shows, geared mainly towards a tourist crowd, hark back to the 'naughty' image of Paris of yesteryear. The Folies Bergères (32 rue Richer), which launched the careers of Josephine Baker, Mistinguett and Maurice Chevalier, and the Lido (116bis avenue des Champs-Elysées) are classic survivors. The Crazy Horse (12 avenue George V) puts on erotic, slickly choreographed shows. The Moulin Rouge (82 boulevard de Clichy) puts on two shows a night.

Clubbing

Keeping up with the latest in clubs can be a full-time job for dedicated night-owls. Many are nominally private, meaning you only get in if your face fits. Some of the more exclusive places are around the Champs-Elysées. Cooler venues tend to come and go in the Bastille/Oberkampf area. The Marais is where to hang out for the gay scene.

CHILDREN

For most children, Disneyland *(see page 86)* will probably appeal far more than city sightseeing. For a cheaper alternative, an afternoon in one of Paris's parks *(see pages 39 and 73)* might do the trick. For small children there are merry-go-rounds, puppet theatres (not July and August), pony rides and toy boats in the **Jardin du Luxembourg**. Animal-loving

In the Jardin du Luxembourg

younsters may like to visit the **Jardin d'Acclimatation** *(see page 59)*, a children's park with a zoo, pony rides and puppet shows in the Bois de Boulogne.

For the scientifically minded, there's a lot to learn in the **Cité des Sciences et de l'Industrie** *(see page 63)*. At the **Palais de la Découverte** *(see page 55)* there's also a hands-on approach.

Calendar of Events

For details of these and other events, see <www.parisinfo.com>.

January Prêt à Porter Paris, the spring ready-to-wear fashion shows at Paris-Expo, Métro: Porte de Versailles. Chinese New Year, Chinatown, 13th *arrondissement*, Métro: Porte d'Ivry.

Spring Foire du Trône (late March–early May), a monster funfair at Pelouse de Reuilly, Bois de Vincennes, Métro: Porte Dorée.

April Paris Marathon ends on the Champs-Elysées.

Good Friday Archbishop of Paris leads Procession of the Cross up the steps of Sacré-Coeur basilica, Montmartre, Métro: Anvers.

May/June French Open Tennis Championships, chic Grand Slam event, Roland-Garros stadium, Métro: Porte d'Auteuil.

June For the Fête de la Musique (Music Festival) on the 21st, there are free concerts all over Paris. The Course des Garçons et Serveuses de Café has 500 waiters and waitresses racing through the *grands boulevards* and St-Germain-des-Prés.

July Bastille Day (14th). Festivities include a colourful military parade along the Champs-Elysées, a firework display at the Trocadéro and dancing on place de la Bastille. The Tour de France ends on the Champs-Elysées. Paris Cinéma, international film festival, screenings at various venues; see <www.paris-cinema.org>. Night-time firework displays and illuminated fountains at the Château de Versailles (July–Sept).

September Journée du Patrimoine, open day at otherwise off-limits government and private buildings.

October Prix de l'Arc de Triomphe, France's biggest horse race, Longchamp, Bois de Boulogne, Métro: Porte d'Auteuil and free shuttle-bus. Festival d'Automne, the annual festival of theatre, music and dance (until December).

November The arrival of Beaujolais Nouveau (third Tuesday of the month) is celebrated in bars and restaurants.

December Notre-Dame cathedral is packed for 11pm Christmas Eve Mass. New Year's Eve crowds pour onto the Champs-Elysées, and there are fireworks at the Trocadéro.

EATING OUT

Paris has the reputation of being one of the best food cities in the world. However, over the past ten years gastronomic critics have been hard on the French capital, claiming that, unlike in London, New York and Sydney, the culinary scene has been stubbornly slow to evolve. 'Duck *à l'orange*, again?' There is some truth to these reproaches – France is conservative when it comes to food – but this attitude is not without benefits, especially for visitors; and, furthermore, in many ways it makes sense.

Classic to Contemporary

The great cuisines of the world can be counted on one hand, and French cuisine is one of them. What the term implies is

Red gingham – traditional French dining

an established, coherent body of ingredients, techniques and dishes, which have all been studied and perfected by masters of the art over many years. So, if a chef doesn't immediately hurl lemongrass into his *coq au vin*, it doesn't necessarily mean that he's unimaginative: it simply means that he

respects tradition and has enough experience with flavour to know that it has its risks. In other words, it could be argued that French cuisine went through its culinary adolescence long ago, and that at this stage there are some taste thrills it considers not worth pursuing.

This is not to say that French food isn't evolving. New flavours are integrated into the cooking all the time, but they are carefully integrated. Curry, lime, peanut, peppers, coconut and lemongrass are all common on gastronomic menus. Most dishes remain French at the core, but exotic nuances are certainly part of the high-end experience. And in the middle ground, couscous is eaten almost as often as *boeuf bourguignon*, and sushi seems to be the city's favourite fast food.

Even in terms of technique, French cooking has modernised; sauces and pastries, for example, tend to be lighter than they were previously, and vegetables are more prevalent on menus. Menus themselves have been simplified – better aligned to contemporary appetites. Still, it's a slow-and-steady-wins-the-race approach to moving cuisine forward.

The advantage of this from a visitor's perspective is that the classic dishes we dream about abroad can still be found in authentic form on French tables. If you want French onion soup, you can find it, plain and simple. If you order *steak au poivre*, out will come that desired slab of beef in a creamy, peppery sauce that spills across the plate towards your crispy pile of *frites*. There are even a few bistros left where old-style service is still the norm, so when you order, say, *mousse au chocolat*, you'll be given a family-sized bowl from which you can serve yourself until you swear that you'll never want to see the dish again as long as you live.

It can all sound very idyllic, but fear not, the dreadful French restaurant experience still exists: the flowery wallpaper, those pink polyester napkins, the huffy waiter, the Côtes du Rhône as cold as the North Atlantic, fish cooked beyond recognition and accompanied by asparagus spears on crutches. There's plenty of mediocrity as far as restaurant food goes, but the French are so French about it all that sometimes even the most ghastly meals can have a certain charm.

Another thing that makes French food extraordinary (and the bad French food, on a gracious day, forgivable) is the degree to which it is social. Occasionally, you'll spot someone dashing along the road nibbling at a falafel, but it's quite rare. Even with the increased pace of modern life, the French still believe in sitting down and sharing meals in good company

Le Fooding

The term 'Le Fooding', coined in 1999 by journalist Alexandre Cammas, joins the two English words 'food' and 'feeling' to express an attitude towards dining that emphasises emotion, atmosphere, alluring food presentation, imagination, entertainment and time, as much as high-quality food on the plate. Says Cammas, 'People need a lot more than just good food to feel well fed.' It's all about approaching the table with the mind and all the senses, not just an empty belly and a greedy tongue. In a way, this is what France has always been famous for. For restaurants that share these ideals, visit <www.lefooding.com>.

over a bottle of wine. They take time to eat – they make time. In fact, food in France, more than just sustenance, is a lifestyle; and this, if nothing else, is something you'll wish you could pack in your bag and take home with you when you leave.

Where to Eat

Eateries in Paris are still by and large French: bistros, brasseries, cafés and haute-cuisine restaurants. Bistros tend to serve simple, traditional dishes. The food quality varies from one to the next, unlike the menus, which are practically carbon copies of each other: eggs

Le Train Bleu at Gare de Lyon

poached in red wine, potato and herring salad, duck confit, beef daube, chocolate mousse and tarte Tatin – over and over and over again. Brasseries (the louder, brighter, Belle Epoque option) offer a range of bistro dishes, but also specialise in seafood – heaps of oysters, mussels, langoustines, lobsters and clams spinning past on waiters' dexterous palms – and Alsatian dishes including choucroute and plenty of beer.

Cafés, in the traditional sense of the term, usually serve sandwiches, notably the ubiquitous *croque-monsieur* (grilled ham and cheese) and a variety of salads. However, modern 'cafés' – trendy, chic establishments that pack in fashionable crowds – serve full menus, typically of contemporary, cosmopolitan food with a Mediterranean bent.

At the high end, Michelin-starred restaurants range from being gloriously old-fashioned, with truffle-studded foie gras terrines and venison in grand old sauces, to being acrobatically cutting-edge with hot pepper sorbets to cleanse the palate between veal slow-cooked in orange juice and desserts that show off milk or chocolate in five different ways. One of the best ways to enjoy the starred places is to opt for a tasting menu *(dégustation)*, which affords you hours at the table tasting a host of dishes in smaller-than-usual portions, so that there's room for them all.

Ethnic Cuisine

If you get to the point where you think you might burst if you have to look at another plate of French food, take a break by seeking out some of the city's international restaurants. What better way to experience the different *quartiers* of Paris than through the city's exceptional – and delicious – culinary scene? Paris is especially good for food from Morocco, other parts of Africa, the Antilles, Thailand, Vietnam and, increasingly, Japan. In terms of location, the greatest concentration of Chinese and Vietnamese restaurants is in the 5th and 13th

Traditional tiles

arrondissements (roughly the Latin Quarter and southeast to the new Left Bank), while Japanese eateries have all but taken over parts of the 1st (around the Louvre, Palais-Royal and Châtelet). The best Moroccan restaurants are peppered across the capital, but around the Bastille is a good place to start. There is excellent Lebanese food in the 8th and 16th (Madeleine,

Art Nouveau décor at Gallopin

Grands Boulevards, Champs-Elysées and West), while good African food can be found around Pigalle and the East. And cheap Indian canteens are concentrated on the streets behind the Gare du Nord in the 10th.

Eating Out with Children
Taking your children out to a restaurant should not be a problem (although check beforehand with the more upmarket places). French children are used to eating out from an early age and are therefore generally well behaved in restaurants. Many establishments offer a children's menu. If not, they may split a *prix-fixe* menu between two. With very young children, just request an extra plate and give them food from your own. Alternatively, order a simple dish from the *à la carte menu*, such as an omelette or soup. With the bread that comes automatically to a French table, and ice-cream or fruit to follow, most children will be well fed.

Le Square Trousseau, in the 12th *arrondissement*

Useful Phrases

Do you have a table?	**Avez-vous une table?**
The bill, please	**L'addition, s'il vous plaît**
I would like…	**J'aimerais…**

To Help You Order…

menu	**la carte**	cheese	**du fromage**
tea	**du thé**	chips (fries)	**des frites**
coffee	**un café**	salt	**du sel**
milk	**du lait**	pepper	**du poivre**
sugar	**du sucre**	salad	**une salade**
wine	**du vin**	soup	**de la soupe**
beer	**une bière**	meat	**de la viande**
glass	**un verre**	fish	**du poisson**
water	**de l'eau**	seafood	**des fruits**
bread	**du pain**		**de mer**
butter	**du beurre**	dessert	**un dessert**

...and Read the Menu

ail	garlic	**jambon**	ham
agneau	lamb	**langouste**	rock lobster
asperges	asparagus	**lapin**	rabbit
bar	sea bass	**moules**	mussels
bœuf	beef	**nouilles**	noodles
caille	quail	**œufs**	eggs
canard	duck	**oignons**	onions
caneton	duckling	**petits pois**	peas
cerises	cherries	**pintade**	guinea fowl
champignons	mushrooms	**poché**	poached
chou	cabbage	**poire**	pear
choufleur	cauliflower	**poireaux**	leeks
crevettes	prawns/	**pomme**	apple
roses/grises	shrimps	**pomme de terre**	potato
crudités	raw vegetables	**porc**	pork
daurade	sea bream	**poulet**	chicken
dinde	turkey	**raisins**	grapes
échalotes	shallots	**ris de veau**	calf's sweetbreads
épinards	spinach		
escargots	snails	**riz**	rice
farci	stuffed	**rognon**	kidney
foie	liver	**rouget**	red mullet
fraises	strawberries	**rôti**	roast
framboises	raspberries	**saucisse**	sausage
grillé	grilled	**saumon**	salmon
haricots verts	green beans	**thon**	tuna
homard	lobster	**truite**	trout
huîtres	oysters	**veau**	veal

And how would you like your meat?

very rare	**bleu**	medium	**à point**
rare	**saignant**	well done	**bien cuit**
medium-rare	**rose**		

HANDY TRAVEL TIPS

An A–Z Summary of Practical Information

A

ACCOMMODATION (see also HOTEL LISTINGS on page 128)

Paris is a popular destination all year round, so booking in advance is recommended in any season. Hotels are officially classified into five categories, from one to five stars, determined by comfort and amenities; a complete booklet is available from the Paris tourist information office. Rates depend on the hotel's amenities and location, and are posted visibly at reception desks.

For a long stay you might consider renting an apartment. Travel sections of national newspapers carry advertisements; the *International Herald Tribune* and FUSAC (France-USA Contacts), available at expatriate hangouts and embassies, list accommodation for rent. **Alcôve & Agapes** (8bis rue Coysevox, 75018, tel: 01 44 85 06 05, <www.bed-and-breakfast-in-paris.com>) organise rooms in private homes.

Do you have a single/double room	Avez-vous une chambre pour une/deux personnes
What's the rate per night?	Quel est le prix pour une nuit?

Camping

The only site reasonably close to the centre of Paris is in the Bois de Boulogne, beside the Seine. Camping du Bois de Boulogne, allée du Bord de l'Eau, 75016, tel: 01 45 24 30 00.

Youth Hostels

A free guide with full information on French youth hostels is available from the Fédération Unie des Auberges de Jeunesse (FUAJ), 27 rue Pajol, 75018 Paris, tel: 01 44 89 87 27 <www.fuaj.org>. Tourist information offices also offer a useful booklet entitled *Jeunes à Paris* (Young People in Paris) with addresses and telephone numbers of hostels, student halls and other low-budget accommodation.

Youth hostels are at the following locations:

- **Auberge Jules Ferry**, 8 bvd Jules-Ferry, 75011; tel: 01 43 57 55 60.
- **Auberge Internationale des Jeunes**, 10 rue Trousseau, 75011; tel: 01 47 00 62 00, <www.aijparis.com>.
- **Centre International de Paris/Louvre** (BVJ), 20 rue Jean-Jacques Rousseau, 75001; tel: 01 53 00 90 90.
- **Le Fauconnier**, 11 rue du Fauconnier, 75004; tel: 01 42 74 23 45.
- **Le Fourcy**, 6 rue de Fourcy, 75004; tel: 01 42 74 23 45.
- **Maubuisson**, 12 rue des Barres, 75004; tel: 01 42 74 23 45.

For further details of Le Fauconnier, Le Fourcy and Maubuisson, see <www.mije.com>.

AIRPORTS (Aéroports)

Paris has two main airports. **Roissy-Charles-de-Gaulle**, about 30 km (19 miles) northeast of the city, and **Orly**, 18 km (11 miles) south.

Charles-de-Gaulle to Central Paris

Train: The quickest way of getting to central Paris from Roissy/ Charles-de-Gaulle is by RER train. These leave every 15 minutes between 5am and 11.45pm from terminal 2 (take the connecting shuttle bus if you arrive at terminal 1) and run to the Métro stops at Gare du Nord or Châtelet. The journey takes about 45 minutes.

Bus: Roissybus runs between the airport and rue Scribe (near the Palais-Garnier) from terminals 1 gate 30, 2A gate 10 and 2D gate 12. It runs every 15 minutes from 5.45am to 11pm and takes 45 to 60 minutes. Alternatively, the Air France bus (to Métro Porte Maillot or Charles-de-Gaulle Etoile) leaves from terminals 2A and 2B or terminal 1, arrival level gate 34. It runs every 12 minutes from 5.45am to 11pm.

Taxis: The journey from Roissy can take anything from around 30 minutes to over an hour, depending on the traffic. The charge is metered, with supplements payable for each large piece of luggage.

Orly to Central Paris

Trains: Take the shuttle from gate H at Orly Sud or arrivals gate F at Orly Ouest to Orly railway station. The RER stops at Austerlitz, Pont St-Michel and the Quai d'Orsay. It runs every 15 minutes from 6am to 11pm and takes around 30 minutes to Austerlitz.

Bus: The Orlybus (to place Denfert-Rochereau) leaves from Orly Sud gate F or Orly Ouest arrivals gate D. It runs around every 10 minutes from 5.35am to 11.05pm. The more expensive **Orlyval** automatic train is a shuttle to Antony (the nearest RER to Orly). It runs every 5–8 minutes from 6am to 11pm daily, and takes 30 minutes.

Air France buses (to Invalides and Gare Montparnasse) leave from Orly Sud gate J, or Orly Ouest arrivals gate E. They run every 15 minutes from 6am to 11pm and take 30 minutes. Tickets are available from the Air France terminus. See also <www.airfrance.fr>.

Taxi: The journey from Orly to the city centre takes 20–40 minutes, depending on the traffic.

B

BICYCLE HIRE (Rental) *(Location de bicyclettes)*

You can rent bikes by the day or week from Paris-Vélo, 2 rue du Fer à Moulin, 75005, tel: 01 43 37 59 22, <www.paris-velo-rent-a-bike.fr>. Paris à Vélo C'est Sympa, 37 boulevard Bourdon, tel: 01 48 87 60 01, fax: 01 48 87 61 01, <www.parisvelosympa.com> also rent bikes.

BUDGETING FOR YOUR TRIP

The price of accommodation varies widely. You can get a double room in a small *pension* for under €50 a night, or you can pay €300 in a luxury hotel. An average price, however, for an en-suite double room in a centrally located, comfortable hotel is around €100–150.

Meals also cover a wide price range, but on average expect to pay around €30–40 for a three-course meal with a half-bottle of house wine. The average entrance price to a national museum or gallery is about €7–8 (municipal ones are free). A taxi from the airport will cost around €45–60, depending on traffic, plus €1 per bag and a tip of about 5 percent. For ticket deals, refer to Transport *(see page 125)*.

(see page 125)

C

CAR HIRE (Rental) *(Location de voitures)*

To rent a car you will need to show your driver's licence (held for at least a year) and passport. You will also need a major credit card, or a large deposit. The minimum age for renting cars is 23, or 21 if paying by credit card. Third-party insurance is compulsory; full cover is recommended. The Yellow Pages *(Pages Jaunes)* lists companies under *Location d'automobiles*.

Among the international car-hire firms operating in Paris are:
Auto Europe, on-line bookings only, <www.autoeurope.com>.
Avis, tel: 08 20 05 05 05, <www.avis.fr>.
Europcar/National/InterRent, tel: 08 25 35 83 58, <www.europcar.fr>.
Hertz, tel: 01 39 38 38 38 <www.hertz.fr>.

| I'd like to rent a car | **Je voudrais louer une voiture** |

CLIMATE

Winter temperatures in Paris average 4°C (39°F), while in summer temperatures average around 25°C (77°F) – with some extreme heats of around 40°C (104°F) in recent years. Spring and autumn tend to be mild, with an average temperature of 11°C (52°F). June, September and October are ideal months for visiting, as they are warm, usually sunny, but less stifling (and crowded) than the mid-summer months.

CLOTHING

Parisians tend to be dressier than Londoners or New Yorkers. In smarter restaurants men may be expected to wear jackets, although ties are rarely insisted upon. A pair of sturdy walking shoes is essential if you plan on seeing the city on foot – the best way to tour Paris. A raincoat is useful in winter, and an umbrella at any time of year.

CRIME AND SAFETY

As in any other major city, it is wise to take sensible precautions with your possessions. There are pickpockets in some Métro stations. Obvious centres of prostitution (such as rue St-Denis and parts of the Bois de Boulogne) are best avoided at night. It's always a good idea to keep a photocopy of your passport in case of theft.

In the event of loss or theft, a report must be made in person at the nearest police station *(commissariat de police)* as soon as possible after the event. This will also be required if you wish to claim from your insurance company. For emergency help, tel: 17.

CUSTOMS AND ENTRY REQUIREMENTS

Nationals of European Union (EU) countries and Switzerland need only a valid passport or identity document to enter France. Nationals from Australia, Canada, New Zealand and the US require passports, while South African nationals need a visa. For the latest information on entry requirements, contact the French embassy in your country.

Since the abolition of duty-free goods within the EU in 1999, there are no limits imposed on the amount of tobacco or alcohol you can take into France if travelling from another EU country. (But you may need to prove at customs that the goods are for your personal use only.)

If you are from a non-EU country and buy goods duty free in France, there are limits on the amount of goods you can take home (these quanties may be doubled if you live outside Europe): 200 cigarettes or 100 cigarillos or 50 cigars or 250g tobacco; 2 litres of wine or 1 litre of spirits; 50g of perfume plus 250ml of eau de toilette.

Currency restrictions: There is no limit on the amount of local or foreign currencies that can be brought into France, from anywhere in the world, but amounts in bank notes exceeding €7,600 (or equivalent) should be declared, if you intend to export them.

D

DISABLED TRAVELLERS

Travellers with mobility problems are advised to book accommodation in advance. Most official lists of hotels use a symbol to denote wheelchair access, but it is always wise to double check with the hotel.

Wheelchairs are available to rent from: **CRF Matériel Médical**, 153 boulevard Voltaire, 75011, tel: 01 43 73 98 98. **Ptitcar**, <www.ptitcar.com>, is an excellent Paris-based company that operates a fleet of wheelchair-accessible vehicles for transport and tours. They also prepare holiday itineraries for wheelchair users.

Useful Organisations
France: Association des Paralysés de France, Service Information, 17 bvd Auguste Blanqui, 75013, tel: 01 40 78 69 00, <www.apf.asso.fr>.

UK: RADAR, The Royal Association for Disability and Rehabilitation, 12 City Forum, 250 City Road, London EC1V 8AF, tel: 020 7250 3222, <www.radar.org.uk>.

US: Society for Accessible Travel and Hospitality (SATH), 347 Fifth Avenue, Suite 610, New York, tel: 212-447 7284, <www.sath.org>.

DRIVING

Driving in Paris requires confidence and concentration. If you do intend to drive, note the following. Seat belts are obligatory in both the front and back of the car, and the speed limit in town is 50kph (30mph). Do not drive in bus lanes at any time, and give priority to

driver's licence	**permis de conduire**
car registration papers	**carte grise**

vehicles approaching from the right. This applies to some round-abouts, where cars on the roundabout stop for those coming on to it. Helmets are compulsory for motorbike riders and passengers. Street parking is very difficult to find; spaces are usually metered Mon–Sat 9am–7pm (paid for with a Paris Carte, currently €10 or €30, purchased from a local *tabac*), and the maximum stay is two hours; most car parks are underground (see <www.parkings deparis.fr>). Illegally parked cars may be towed away. Do not leave any possessions on show, as theft from cars is common.

Petrol can be hard to find in the city centre, so if your tank is almost empty head for a *porte* (exit) on the Périphérique (the multi-lane ring road), where petrol stations are open 24 hours a day all year round.

Drivers are liable to heavy on-the-spot fines for speeding and drunk driving. The drink limit in France is 50mg/litre of alcohol in the blood (equivalent to about two glasses of wine) and is strictly enforced.

Priorité à droite	Yield to traffic from right
Ralentir	Slow down
Serrez à droite/à gauche	Keep right/left
Sens unique	One way
Vous n'avez pas la priorité	Give way

E

ELECTRICITY

You'll need an adapter for most British and US plugs: French sockets have two round holes. Supplies are 220 volt, and US equipment will need a transformer. Shaver outlets are generally dual voltage.

EMBASSIES AND CONSULATES

Australia 4 rue Jean-Rey, 75015, tel: 01 40 59 33 00
Canada 35 avenue Montaigne, 75008, tel: 01 44 43 29 00
New Zealand 7ter rue Léonard-de-Vinci, 75016, tel: 01 45 01 43 43
Republic of Ireland Embassy: 12 avenue Foch, 75016, tel: 01 44 17 67 00. Consulate: 4 rue Rude, 75016
UK Embassy: 35 rue du Faubourg-St-Honoré, 75008, tel: 01 44 51 32 81. Consulate: 18bis rue d'Anjou, 75008, tel: 01 44 51 31 02
US Embassy: 2 avenue Gabriel, 75001, tel: 01 43 12 22 22
Consulate: 2 rue St-Florentin, 75001, tel: 08 36 70 14 88

EMERGENCIES *(Urgence)*

Emergency telephone numbers:

Ambulance *(SAMU)*	15
Police *(police secours)*	17
Fire brigade *(sapeurs-pompiers)*	18
From a mobile phone:	112

Police!	**Police!**
Fire!	**Au feu!**
Help!	**Au secours!**

G

GAY AND LESBIAN TRAVELLERS

The city has a large, visible and quite relaxed gay community. Gay bars and clubs are concentrated around the Marais. The magazine *Têtu*, available at kiosks, is a useful source of information.

GETTING THERE (see also AIRPORTS)

By Air: Air France is the main agent for flights to France from the US and within Europe and also handles bookings for some of the smaller operators, such as Brit Air. For British travellers, operators such as British Airways and the low-cost airlines easyJet and British Midland offer flights to Paris from London and other British cities.

By Sea: Ferries from the UK, Ireland and Channel Islands to the northern ports of France have reduced their prices since the Channel Tunnel opened. Seacat catamarans offer the fastest service but are subject to cancellation if the sea is very rough. There are motorway links from Boulogne, Calais and Le Havre to Paris.

The following operate from the UK/Ireland: **Condor Ferries** (tel: 0870 243 5140, <www.condorferries.co.uk>) sail from Weymouth to St Malo and Portsmouth to Cherbourg. **Hoverspeed** (tel: 0870 164 2114, <www.hoverspeed.com>) runs a two-hour Superseacat service from Newhaven to Dieppe and a one-hour Seacat service from Dover to Calais. **P&O Ferries** (tel: 0870 598 0333, <www.poferries.com>) sails from Dover to Calais and Portsmouth to Le Havre and Cherbourg. **SeaFrance** (tel: 0871 663 2546, <www.seafrance.com>) sails from Dover to Calais. **Speed Ferries** (tel: 0870 220 0570, <www.speedferries.com>) offers a 50-minute crossing from Dover to Boulogne. **Irish Ferries** (tel: 08705 171 1717, <www.irishferries.com>) runs services from Rosslaire and Cork to Le Havre and Cherbourg.

By Rail: The Eurostar has fast, frequent rail services from London (St Pancras International), Ebbsfleet or Ashford to Paris (Gare du Nord). The service runs about 12 times a day and takes two and a quarter hours (two hours from Ebbsfleet). For reservations, contact Eurostar on tel: 0870 518 6186 (UK) or 08 92 35 35 39 (France) or visit <www.eurostar.com>. There are reduced fares for children aged 4–11; those under 3 travel free but are not guaranteed a seat.

By Car: For those coming from the UK by car, Eurotunnel takes cars and passengers from Folkestone to Calais on a drive-on, drive-off service, known as Le Shuttle. It takes 35 minutes from platform to platform and about one hour from motorway to motorway. Payment is made at toll booths, which accept cash, cheques or credit cards. The price applies to the car, regardless of the number of passengers or car size. You can book in advance with Eurotunnel on tel: 0870 535 3535 (UK) or 08 10 63 03 04 (France) or at <www.eurotunnel.com>. Alternatively, you can just turn up and take the next available service. Le Shuttle runs 24 hours a day, all year, and there are between two and five an hour, depending on the season and time of day.

By Bus: National Express Eurolines runs services from London (Victoria Coach Station) to Paris daily, providing one of the cheaper ways to get to the French capital. Discounts are available for under-26s and senior citizens, and the ticket includes the ferry crossing (via Dover). For more information contact National Express Eurolines at 4 Cardiff Road, Luton, Bedfordshire, LU1 1PP, tel: 0870 580 8080, <www.nationalexpress.com>, or Eurolines France, at the Gare Routière-Coach Station Gallieni, 28 avenue du Général de Gaulle, 93170 Bagnolet (Métro Gallieni), tel: 08 36 69 52 52, or visit <www.eurolines.com>.

GUIDES AND TOURS

Find multilingual guides and interpreters through the Office de Tourisme de Paris *(see page 124)*. Their monthly booklet *Paris Sélection* lists telephone contacts. For something a little different, try a tour on a Segway, a quirky motorised scooter-style vehicle. See <www.citysegwaytours.com/paris> for more details.

H

HEALTH AND MEDICAL CARE (see also EMERGENCIES)

EU Nationals: If you are an EU national and you fall ill in France, you can receive emergency medical treatment from doctors, dentists and hospitals. You will have to pay the cost of this treatment, but are entitled to claim from the French Sécurité Sociale, which refunds up to 70 percent of your medical expenses. To receive a refund you must have a European Health Insurance Card. For UK citizens, these are available by going online at <www.dh.gov.uk> or from post offices.

For more information, consult the leaflet *Health Advice for Travellers* (available from post offices, online at <www.dh.gov.uk> or by tel: 020 7210 4850).

North American Citizens: In North America, contact the International Association for Medical Assistance to Travellers (IAMAT), 40 Regal Road, Guelph, Ontario N1K 1B5, Canada, tel: 519 836 0102. This is a non-profit-making group that offers members fixed rates for medical treatment from participating physicians. Members receive a passport-sized medical record completed by their doctor and a directory of English-speaking IAMAT doctors in France, who are on call 24 hours a day. Membership is free, but a donation is requested.

In Paris, English-speaking health services are at the private American Hospital, tel: 01 46 41 25 25, <www.american-hospital.org>.

Chemists (Drugstores): Pharmacie des Halles, 10 boulevard de Sébastopol, 75004 (Métro Châtelet), tel: 01 42 72 03 23, is open 9am–midnight, Mon–Sat, and 9am–10pm on Sun. Publicis Drugstore, 133 avenue des Champs-Elysées, 75008 (Métro Etoile), tel: 01 47 20 39 25, is open Mon–Fri 8am–2am, Sat–Sun 10am–2pm.

HOLIDAYS *(Jours fériés)*

Public offices, banks and most shops close on public holidays, though you'll find the odd corner shop open. If one of these days falls on a Tuesday or Thursday, many working people take the Monday or Friday off as well for a long weekend (though this doesn't usually curtail activity in shops or businesses).

1 January	*Jour de l'An*	New Year's Day
1 May	*Fête du Travail*	Labour Day

8 May	*Fête de la Victoire*	Victory Day (1945)
14 July	*Fête Nationale*	Bastille Day
15 August	*Assomption*	Assumption
1 November	*Toussaint*	All Saints' Day
11 November	*Armistice*	Armistice Day (1918)
25 December	*Noël*	Christmas Day

Moveable dates:

Lundi de Pâques	Easter Monday
Ascension	Ascension Day
Lundi de Pentecôte	Whit Monday

L

LANGUAGE

Even if your French isn't perfect, don't feel inhibited: it's better to try a few words, and your efforts will be appreciated by Parisians. You cannot assume people speak English.

The *Berlitz French Phrase Book and Dictionary* covers almost all the situations you are likely to encounter in your travels.

LOST PROPERTY

If your personal documents, cash, belongings or travellers' cheques are lost or stolen, go to the Commissariat de Police closest to the scene of the crime as soon as possible. If you lose your passport, report it to your consulate (*see page 114* or the *Pages Blanches* and *Pages Jaunes* phone books under 'Ambassades et Consulats'; also <www.pagesjaunes.fr>), as soon as possible.

If your credit card is lost or stolen, the numbers to ring are:
American Express, tel: 01 47 77 70 00
Visa or **Carte Bleue** and **Mastercard-Eurocard**, tel: 08 36 69 08 80

To reclaim anything else you have lost, you should go (with ID) to the Bureau des Objets Trouvés, 36 rue des Morillons, 75732

Cedex 15, tel: 08 21 00 25 25 (Métro Convention), open weekdays 8.30am–5pm, except Fri, when it shuts at 4.30pm. You need to visit the office in person, as no information is given over the telephone.

M

MAPS

Paris Pratique par Arrondissement, an indexed, pocket-sized street-atlas, is the most useful map for visitors. It can be bought for around €6 at newsstands and kiosks across the city. Free city street maps are supplied by tourist information offices. Most Métro stations supply decent maps of the Métro system, bus network and RER train system.

MEDIA

Newspapers: The two main national dailies are *Le Monde*, which has a dry, leftish slant, and the more conservative *Le Figaro*. The paper representing the Communist Party is *L'Humanité*, and not veering quite so heavily left is the paper Jean-Paul Sartre helped to found, *Libération*. France's biggest-selling daily is *France-Soir*. The major weekly news publications are *Le Point* (right), *L'Express* (centre) and *Le Nouvel Observateur* (left). British, American and other European dailies are widely available on the same day at city-centre kiosks and shops showing *journaux* or *presse* signs.

For cultural listings, read the weekly *L'Officiel des Spectacles* or *Pariscope*, both published on Wednesdays.

Radio: France Inter (87.8 MHz) is the main national radio station, with a lot of serious discussion. Radio Classique (101.1 MHz) plays uninterrupted lightweight classical music. For something less mainstream, try France Musiques (91.7 and 92.1 MHz). RTL (104.3 MHz) is the most popular station throughout France, playing music from the charts, interspersed with chat shows. Europe 1 (104.7 FM) is good for morning news. France Info (105.5 FM) is a non-stop news channel.

Television: TF1, France 2, France 3, France 5/Arte and M6 are the five main television stations on offer. There is also a huge choice of cable channels. Canal+ is a subscription channel, which shows big-name new releases and also helps fund film production.

MONEY

Currency: The euro (€) is divided into 100 cents (¢ or ct). Coins *(pièces)* come in 1, 2, 5, 10, 20 and 50 cents, and 1 and 2 euros. Banknotes *(billets)* come in 5, 10, 20, 50, 100, 200 and 500 euros.

Banks and currency exchange offices *(banque; bureau de change)*: Take your passport when you go to change money or travellers' cheques. Your hotel may also offer an exchange service, though typically at a less favourable rate than a bank.

I want to change some pounds/dollars	**Je voudrais changer des livres sterling/dollars**
Do you accept travellers' cheques/this credit card?	**Acceptez-vous les chèques de voyage/cette carte de crédit?**

Credit cards: The majority of large shops and restaurants, and almost all hotels, accept credit cards. The most common in France are Visa and Carte Bleue (often referred to as 'CB'). American Express (Amex), Diner's Club (DC) and Mastercard are widely recognised, and many places also now accept Maestro and Cirrus. However, if you don't see your card's sticker in the hotel, shop or restaurant window, it's always advisable to ask first whether you can use it.

Travellers' cheques: These are widely accepted (with identification).

Sales tax: Value-added tax (TVA) of 19.6 percent is imposed on almost all goods and services, and usually included in the price. Visitors from non-EU countries can have the TVA refunded on goods bought for export.

O

OPENING HOURS *(horaires d'ouverture)*

Office workers normally start early (8.30am is not uncommon) and often stay at their desks until 6pm or later. This is partly to make up for the long lunch hours (two hours, from around noon) that are traditional in public offices. Some companies are changing to shorter lunch breaks, as employees appreciate the advantages of getting home earlier in the evening. Traditionally, banks open Monday to Friday 9am–5.30pm and close on Saturday and Sunday. However, many banks now open on Saturday morning and close on Monday instead.

Food shops, especially bakers, tend to open early. Most boutiques and department stores open about 9am, although some do not open until 10am. Traditionally in France most shops close from around noon to 2.30pm, but in Paris, many remain open until 7 or 7.30pm. The larger department stores do not close at lunchtime and are open until 9 or 10pm on Thursday. Most shops close on Sunday, although bakers and patisseries are usually open in the morning.

Are you open tomorrow?	**Est-ce que vous ouvrez demain?**

P

POLICE *(see also EMERGENCIES)*

The blue-uniformed police who keep law and order and direct traffic are, as a general rule, courteous and helpful to visitors. The CRS *(Compagnies républicaines de sécurité)* are the tough guys, seen wielding batons to deal with demonstrations. Outside Paris and other main cities, the *gendarmes*, in blue trousers and black jackets

with white belts, are responsible for traffic and crime investigation.
If you need to call for police help, dial 17 (anywhere in France).

Where's the nearest police station?	**Où se trouve le commissariat de police le plus proche?**

POST OFFICES *(bureau de poste)*

The French post office is run by the PTT (Poste et Télécommunications). The main branches are open Monday to Friday 8am–7pm, Saturday 8am–noon. The central post office, at 52 rue du Louvre, 75001, tel: 01 40 28 76 00, <www.laposte.fr>, operates a daily 24-hour service. Internet, fax and photocopying facilities are available here, as they are in all larger post offices. Stamps *(timbres)* are available at most *tabacs* (tobacconists).

R

RELIGION

The majority of people in Paris are nominally Roman Catholic. However, France has the largest Muslim population in Europe, and Europe's largest Jewish community outside of Russia, of which around 200,000 live in Paris. The city is home to only a few Protestants, and Eastern Orthodox believers are a vanishing minority. The Yellow Pages *(Les Pages Jaunes)*, found in most hotel rooms and at all hotel desks, lists places of worship for every faith and denomination.

T

TELEPHONES *(téléphones)*

All telephone numbers in France have 10 digits. Paris and Ile de France numbers begin with 01. Toll-free phone numbers begin with 0800; all other numbers beginning with 08 are charged at variable rates; and 06 numbers are mobile numbers. There are two kinds of phone boxes in Paris from which you can make local and international calls: coin-operated phones and the more common, card-operated ones. You get 50 percent more call-time for your money if you ring between 10.30pm and 8am on weekdays, and from 2pm at weekends. A *télécarte* can be bought at various prices from kiosks, *tabacs* and post offices. Note that you can only receive telephone calls at telephone boxes displaying a blue bell sign.

You can also dial from all post offices, which have both coin- and card-operated phones. To call long distance, ask at one of the counters and you will be assigned a booth – you pay when your call is over. Cafés and tabacs often also have public phones, which usually take either coins or *jetons*, coin-like discs bought at the bar.

Direct Dialling to Paris from the UK: 00 (international code) + 33 (France) + 1 (Paris) + an eight-figure number. To call other countries from France, first dial the international access code (00), then the country code: Australia 61, UK 44, USA and Canada 1. If using a US credit phone card, call the company's access number: Sprint, tel: 08 00 99 00 87; AT&T, tel: 08 00 99 00 11; MCI, tel: 08 00 99 00 19.
Directory Enquiries: 118712 (France Télécom), 118218 or 118000; for a full list of 118 numbers see <www.appel118.fr>.
Operator: 3123

TIME DIFFERENCES

France keeps to Central European Time (GMT +1 hour; GMT +2 hours Apr–Oct). When it is noon in Paris, it is 6am in New York.

What time is it?	**Quelle heure est-il?**

TIPPING

By law, restaurant bills must include the service charge, usually 12 or 15 percent. Nevertheless, it is common to leave a small additional tip (no more than 5 percent) for the waiter, if the service has been good. With taxis, it's usual to round up to the nearest euro.

TOURIST INFORMATION *(office de tourisme)*

In the UK:
French Travel Centre, 178 Piccadilly, London W1J 9AL, tel: 0906 824 4123 (calls cost 60p per minute), <www.franceguide.com>. Open Mon–Fri 10–6pm, Sat 10am–5pm.

In the US:
Maison de la France (MDLF), 444 Madison Avenue, NY-10022, tel: 514 288 1904. Also 9454 Wilshire Boulevard, Suite 715, 90212, Beverly Hills, CA, tel: 514 288 1904. Consulate General of France, 205 N. Michigan Avenue, Suite 3770, 60601 Chicago, tel: 514 288 1904, <www.franceguide.com>.

In Paris:
• 25 rue des Pyramides, 75001. Open daily 9am–7pm, tel: 08 92 68 30 00, <www.parisinfo.com>
• Carrousel du Louvre, 99 rue de Rivoli, 75001. Open daily 10am–7pm.
• Eiffel Tower, between the east and north pillars. Open May–Sept daily 11am–6.40pm.
• 11 rue Scribe, 75009. Open Mon–Sat 9am–6.30pm.
• 18 rue de Dunkerque, 75010. Open daily 8am–6pm.
• 20 boulevard Diderot, 75012. Open Mon–Sat 8am–6pm.
• 21 place du Tertre, 75018. Open daily 10am–7pm.

TRANSPORT

Bus *(autobus)*: Bus transport around Paris is efficient, though not always fast. Stops are marked by green and blue signs or shelters, with the bus numbers clearly posted, and you'll find bus itineraries displayed under bus shelters. You can obtain a general bus route plan from

Métro station ticket offices. Most buses run 7am–8.30pm, some until 12.30am. Service is reduced on Sundays and public holidays. A special night bus, the Noctambus, runs along 10 main routes serving the capital, from 1.30am–5.30am every hour, with Châtelet as the hub.

Bus journeys take one ticket. You can buy a ticket as you board, but it's cheaper to buy a book of tickets *(carnet)* from any Métro station or tobacconist. (Bus and Métro tickets are interchangeable.) Punch your ticket in the validating machine when you get on. You can also buy special one-, three- or five-day tourist passes or the weekly ticket and *Carte Orange (see below)*. Show these special tickets to the driver as you get on, rather than putting them in the punching machine. The fine for being caught without a ticket is €20.

Métro: The Paris Métropolitain ('Métro' for short) is one of the fastest, most efficient underground railway systems in the world. It's also one of the least expensive. You get 10 journeys for the price of seven by investing in a *carnet* (book) of tickets, also valid for the bus network and – provided that you stay within Paris and don't go to outer suburbs – for the RER.

Express lines (RER, *Réseau Express Régional*) get you into the centre of Paris from the distant suburbs in approximately 15 minutes, with a few stops in between.

A special ticket called **Paris Visite**, valid for three or five days, allows unlimited travel on the bus or Métro, and reductions on entrance fees to various attractions. A **day ticket**, *Forfait 1 Jour Mobilis*, is valid for the Métro, RER, buses, suburban trains and some airport buses.

For longer stays, the best buy is a **Carte Orange** (orange card), valid for unlimited rides inside Paris on the Métro and bus, either weekly *(hebdomadaire)* Mon–Sun, or monthly *(mensuel)* from the first of the month. Ask for a *pochette* (wallet) to go with it and have a passport photo ready.

Whatever your ticket, remember to collect it after putting it through the machine at the Métro entrance gates.

Métro stations have big, easy-to-read maps. Services start at 5.30am and finish around 1am (last trains leave end stations at 12.30am). The RATP (Paris transport authority) has an information office at 54 quai de la Rapée, 75012 Paris. You can call them 24 hours a day on tel: 08 00 15 11 11 or visit <www.ratp.fr>.

Train (train): The SNCF (French railway authority) runs fast, comfortable trains on an efficient network. The **high-speed service** (TGV – *train à grande vitesse*) operating on selected routes is excellent, but more expensive than the average train. Seat reservation is obligatory on TGVs. See <www.sncf.com> or <www.voyages-sncf.com>.

The main stations in Paris are: Gare du Nord (Eurostar to London, and for Belgium and the Netherlands); Gare de l'Est (eastern France and Germany); Gare St-Lazare (Normandy); Gare d'Austerlitz (southwestern France and Spain); Gare Montparnasse (TGV to western and southwestern France); and Gare de Lyon (Provence, Switzerland and Italy). The TGV station at Charles-de-Gaulle Airport also serves Disneyland Paris.

Validate your train ticket before boarding by inserting it in one of the orange machines (called a *machine à composter* or *composteur*) on the way to the platform. If your ticket is not clipped and dated, the inspector is entitled to fine you on the train.

Taxi (taxi): Taxis are generally reasonably priced, though there are extra charges for putting luggage in the boot (trunk) and for pick-up at a station or airport. Taxi drivers can refuse to carry more than three passengers. The fourth, when admitted, pays a supplement.

You'll find taxis cruising around or at stands all over the city. You can recognise an unoccupied cab by an illuminated sign on its roof. Fares differ according to the zones covered or the time of the day (you'll be charged more between 7pm and 7am and on Sunday). An average fare between Roissy-Charles-de-Gaulle Airport and central Paris might be €40 by day, €50 at night. If you have any problems with a driver, you can register a complaint with the Service des Taxis, 36 rue des Morillons, 75015 Paris; tel: 01 53 71 53 71.

The following taxi companies take phone bookings 24 hours a day:

Alpha: 01 45 85 85 85
Artaxi: 08 91 70 25 50
G7: 01 47 39 47 39
Taxis Bleus: 08 25 16 10 10.

W

WEBSITES

Many useful websites are included throughout this guidebook. The following additional sites are only the tip of the iceberg:

www.parisinfo.com official site of the Paris Tourist Office; provides information on hotels, sites, events, exhibitions, transport, weather and more

www.franceguide.com official site of the French Tourist Office, Maison de la France, for general information on France

www.paris.org general information on Paris

www.magicparis.com travel, shops, hotels, etc

www.ratp.fr the official Paris transport site

www.culture.fr official site of the Ministry of Culture

www.rmn.fr guide to national museum exhibitions

www.meteo.fr the weather on-line

www.pagesjaunes.fr the French *Yellow Pages*

www.monuments-nationaux.fr guide to national monuments

www.paris.fr site of the Mairie de Paris, the municipality

WEIGHTS AND MEASURES

The metric system – a French invention – is universally used.

1 kilometre	=	1094 yards or approx 0.6 mile
1 kilogram	=	approx 2.2 lb
1 litre	=	1.75 pint

Recommended Hotels

This list is divided geographically into areas, covering hotels on the islands and the Right and Left banks. Note that the numbers in the postcode indicate the *arrondissement* (district), eg 75004 is the 4th *arrondissement*. Not all properties are wheelchair-accessible – even if a hotel does have an elevator, for example, it's likely that it'll be a fairly small one. Travellers with disabilities should check facilities before reserving.

The following ranges give an idea of the price for a double room per night, with private bath, unless otherwise stated. Service and tax are included; generally, breakfast is not. Note that prices can vary widely within a hotel, and may change according to the time of year. Rooms are often less expensive in August, when Parisians traditionally take a month of holiday. Always confirm the price when booking.

€€€€€	over 375 euros
€€€€	240–375 euros
€€€	115–240 euros
€€	65–115 euros
€	below 65 euros

THE ISLANDS

Hôtel des Deux-Iles €€€ *59 rue St-Louis-en-l'Ile, 75004, tel: 01 43 26 13 35, fax: 01 43 29 60 25, <www.deuxiles-paris-hotel.com>.* Set in a small and attractive 17th-century mansion on the main street of the tranquil Ile St-Louis, this hotel, with just 17 rooms, is comfortable and friendly, with a cellar bar and a vaulted breakfast room with stone walls. Rooms are compact but attractively decorated. Equipped with Wi-Fi.

Hôtel du Jeu de Paume €€€ *54 rue St-Louis-en-l'Ile, 75004, tel: 01 43 26 14 18, fax: 01 40 46 02 76, <www.jeudepaumehotel. com>.* Delightfully set on the pretty Ile St-Louis, this hotel has kept its ancient, 17th-century *jeu de paume* (the predecessor of tennis) court. Great for a taste of old Paris and just steps to Notre-Dame. 30 rooms.

Hôtel de Lutèce €€€ *65 rue St-Louis-en-l'Ile, 75004, tel: 01 43 26 23 52, fax: 01 43 29 60 25, <www.deuxiles-paris-hotel.com>*. On the exclusive Ile St-Louis, this lovely hotel – which is under the same management as the Deux Iles *(see page 128)* – has 23 pretty, tiny rooms that are attractive and very quiet. Those on the sixth floor are the most romantic. Wi-Fi access.

THE RIGHT BANK

LOUVRE AND TUILERIES

Hôtel Costes €€€€€ *239 rue St-Honoré, 75001, tel: 01 42 44 50 00, fax: 01 45 44 50 01, <www.hotelcostes.com>*. This super-hip hotel is just off elegant place Vendôme in this exclusive neighbourhood lined with chic boutiques. The rooms are exquisitely decorated with baroque paintings, heavy drapes and antiques. Some bathrooms have claw-foot bath-tubs and mosaic tiles. Owner Jean-Louis Costes dislikes artificial light, so the hallways are lit with candles; even the beautiful indoor pool is dark. The Café Costes is one of the trendiest places in town. 83 rooms.

Hôtel de Crillon €€€€€ *10 place de la Concorde, 75008, tel: 01 44 71 15 00, fax: 01 44 71 15 02, <www.crillon.com>*. This palatial, world-renowned hotel forms part of the splendid neoclassical façade that dominates the north side of place de la Concorde. Known for its impeccable service and quality, it also has a celebrated bar and two notable restaurants, Michelin-starred Les Ambassadeurs (headed by chef Jean-François Piège) and the more affordable L'Obélisque. There's also the romantic Winter Garden, for tea, coffee and cocktails.

Henri IV € *25 place Dauphine, 75001, tel: 01 43 54 44 53, no fax*. Some of the least-expensive rooms in Paris can be found at this modest budget hotel that has been popular with visiting students for decades. The excellent location is on the delightful place Dauphine across from Ile St-Louis. The 21 rooms are somewhat old-fashioned, with shared bathrooms. Only a short walk from Notre-Dame and St-Michel. Reserve well in advance. No credit cards.

GRANDS BOULEVARDS

Hôtel Chopin € *46 passage Jouffroy, 75009, tel: 01 47 70 58 10, fax: 01 42 47 00 70, <www.hotelbretonnerie.com/chopin.htm>.* Set at the end of an historic 19th-century glass-and-steel-roofed arcade, this is a quiet, friendly, simply furnished hotel. A fabulous price for the location. Book well in advance to stand a chance of staying in one of the 36 rooms.

Claridge Bellman €€€–€€€€ *37 rue François-1er, 75008, tel: 01 47 23 54 42, fax: 01 47 23 08 84, <www.hotelclaridgebellman. com>.* A small boutique hotel offering the personal touch at decent rates in the stylish district lying between the Seine and the avenue des Champs-Elysées. The rooms are attractively furnished with antiques. No restaurant.

Hôtel Edouard VII €€€–€€€€ *39 avenue de l'Opéra, 75002, tel: 01 42 61 56 90, fax: 01 42 61 47 73, <www.edouard7hotel.com>.* Historic, family-owned hotel on one of the grandest avenues in Paris, just a stone's throw from the Palais Garnier and the Louvre. Some rooms at the front have balconies with marvellous views of the opera house. The hotel features the swish Angl'Opéra restaurant *(see page 136)* and a smart, comfortable bar.

Four Seasons George V €€€€€ *31 avenue George V, 75008, tel: 01 49 52 70 00, fax: 01 49 52 71 10, <www.fourseasons.com/ paris>.* One of the most prestigious addresses in Paris, just off the Champs-Elysées. The George V offers the height of opulence, with beautifully classic rooms with modern touches and magnificent marble bathrooms. Exquisite service, and a fabulous spa.

Plaza Athénée €€€€€ *25 avenue Montaigne, 75008, tel: 01 53 67 66 65, fax: 01 53 67 66 66, <www.plaza-athenee-paris.com>.* This palatial hotel, with lavish Versace decor, has soundproofed rooms, a club, restaurant and suites furnished in Louis XVI or Regency style. Super-chef Alain Ducasse is in charge of the restaurant *(see page 136)*. If you can't stretch to the price of a room, treat yourself to a cocktail in the fashionable bar.

Ritz €€€€€ *15 place Vendôme, 75001, tel: 01 43 16 30 30, fax: 01 43 16 31 78, <www.ritzparis.com>*. One of the most prestigious addresses in the world, the Ritz has been associated with the rich and famous for over 100 years. Rooms are plush, decorated in Louis XV style with antique clocks and rich tapestries; many have fireplaces. The spa has a beautiful indoor pool; there are two fine restaurants, the famous Hemingway bar and a pleasant garden.

BEAUBOURG, MARAIS AND BASTILLE

Hôtel Bourg Tibourg €€€ *19 rue du Bourg-Tibourg, 75004, tel: 01 42 78 47 39, fax: 01 40 29 07 00, <www.hotelbourgtibourg. com>*. Situated on a charming narrow street in the heart of the Marais, this 17th-century building is home to a well-kept, affordable boutique hotel. Rooms are warmly decorated with cheery yellow or red wallpaper. Breakfast is served in a vaulted dining room with exposed stone. 31 rooms.

Hôtel Duo €€€ *11 rue du Temple, 75004, tel: 01 42 72 72 22, fax: 01 42 72 03 53, <www.duoparis.com>*. Excellently located trendy hotel in the Marais. Rooms are furnished in the contemporary style, with good-sized bathrooms. There's a bar downstairs, and a gym.

Hôtel de la Place des Vosges €€€ *12 rue Birague, 75004, tel: 01 42 72 60 46, fax: 01 42 72 02 64, <www.hotelplacedesvosges.com>*. An intimate, carefully renovated hotel in a former stables with only 16 rooms. It's popular and in a great location, so book ahead.

Pavillon de la Reine €€€€ *28 place des Vosges, 75003, tel: 01 40 29 19 19, fax: 01 40 29 19 20, <www.pavillon-de-la-reine.com>*. This romantic, mid-sized hotel, located on the beautiful place des Vosges, feels like a country château. Rooms vary greatly in size and price, but most have four-poster beds, exposed wooden beams and antiques. There's also a cosy lobby bar with evening wine-tasting, and manicured gardens.

Hôtel St-Merry €€€ *78 rue de la Verrerie, 75004, tel: 01 42 78 14 15, fax: 01 40 29 06 82, <www.hotelmarais.com>*. One of the most unusual hotels in Paris and once a 17th-century presbytery. Rooms have stained-glass windows and are decorated with mahogany church pews and iron candelabra and, in one, a carved-stone flying buttress. The phone booth is in a confessional. A Gothic masterpiece.

WESTERN PARIS

Hôtel Keppler €€€€ *10 rue Keppler, 75016, tel: 01 47 20 65 05, fax: 01 47 23 02 29, <www.hotelkeppler.com>.* Some of the best accommodation for the price in this posh neighbourhood. The 49 rooms are large and furnished comfortably; four have balconies. There is a spiral staircase, welcoming fireplace and a bar with room service. An impeccably managed, family-owned hotel.

MONTMARTRE

Hôtel Ermitage €€ *24 rue Lamarck, 75018, tel: 01 42 64 79 22, fax: 01 42 64 10 33.* This small hotel is located close to Sacré-Cœur in an old residential neighbourhood. An excellent budget choice, with friendly staff and colourful bedrooms decorated in French farmhouse style. There's a lovely courtyard and terrace, where breakfast is served in summer. 12 rooms. No credit cards.

THE LEFT BANK

LATIN QUARTER AND ST-GERMAIN-DES-PRÉS

Abbaye St-Germain €€€ *10 rue Cassette, 75006, tel: 01 45 44 38 11, fax: 01 45 48 07 86, <www.hotel-abbaye.com>.* This 17th-century abbey, attractively situated between the Jardin du Luxembourg and St-Germain-des-Prés, has been beautifully adapted into a hotel. The charm of the old decor has been maintained – some of the 46 rooms have beams – but there are all mod cons. Lovely garden too. A favourite haunt of writers and artists. Staff are helpful and attentive.

Hôtel d'Angleterre €€€ *44 rue Jacob, 75006, tel: 01 42 60 34 72, fax: 01 42 60 16 93, <www.hotel-dangleterre.com>.* The location couldn't be better, on a quiet, upmarket street lined with art galleries. This lovely hotel was the site at which the Treaty of Paris, proclaiming the independence of the US, was signed in 1783; in the 19th century it was used as the British Embassy. Ernest Hemingway lodged here (in room 14) in 1921. Rooms are fairly small and furnished with antiques; only the top-floor doubles are spacious. Delightful terrace and garden.

Hôtel Familia €€ *11 rue des Ecoles 75005, tel: 01 43 54 55 27, fax: 01 43 29 61 77, <www.hotel-paris-familia.com>.* Location is one of the strong points of this hotel, which is within a few minutes' walk of the islands and St-Germain-des-Prés. The Familia offers solid comforts in smallish rooms for a modest price; rooms on the fifth and sixth floors have views of Notre-Dame. Another attraction for the hotel's many regular guests is the hospitable Gaucheron family who live on the premises and take pride in every detail. Look out for the frescoes painted by a local artist. 30 rooms.

Hôtel des Grandes Ecoles €€–€€€ *75 rue du Cardinal-Lemoine, 75005, tel: 01 43 26 79 23, fax: 01 43 25 28 15, <www.hotel-grandes-ecoles.com>.* At first glance, you might think you were in the French countryside here. There are 50 large, prettily furnished rooms around a cobbled courtyard and garden of established trees and trellised roses. Although it is a short uphill walk from the Métro, you are still near enough to attractions including rue Mouffetard.

Hôtel de Nesle € *7 rue de Nesle, 75006, tel: 01 43 54 62 41.* A laid-back students' and backpackers' hotel. Facilities are basic, but bedrooms are cheerfully decorated with murals, furnished to various eclectic themes and spotless. There is also a garden with a pond and an impressive palm tree.

Hôtel Le Sainte-Beuve €€€ *9 rue Sainte-Beuve, 75006, tel: 01 45 48 20 07, fax: 01 45 48 67 52, <www.hotel-sainte-beuve.fr>.* On a quiet street, steps from the excellent shops on rue d'Assas and a short walk from the Jardin du Luxembourg. The rooms are tastefully furnished, with air-conditioning; those on the top floor have skylights in the bathrooms and romantic views over the rooftops.

AROUND THE EIFFEL TOWER

Amélie €€ *5 rue Amélie, 75007, tel: 01 45 51 74 75, fax: 01 45 56 93 55, <www.hotelamelie-paris.com>*. A short walk from the Eiffel Tower, this small, friendly family-run hotel has some of the lowest rates in the area. Renovated rooms have small refrigerators and private bathrooms. A narrow wooden staircase leads up to the four levels of rooms; there's no lift. Breakfast is served in the small lobby.

Bourgogne et Montana €€€ *3 rue de Bourgogne, 75007, tel: 01 45 51 20 22, fax: 01 45 56 11 98, <www.bourgogne-montana.com>*. A lovely hotel in a building dating from 1789, tucked away behind the Musée d'Orsay. The 30 or so modern, spacious rooms are good value for this pricey neighbourhood. The large doubles are worth the extra splurge and come with double basins as well as antiques.

Hôtel Lenox €€€ *9 rue de l'Université, 75007, tel: 01 42 96 10 95, fax: 01 42 61 52 83, <www.lenoxsaintgermain.com>*. This trendy hotel is decorated in Art Deco style and is very popular among style-conscious types. There's a bar, and the rooms are spotless. Reserve well in advance.

Hôtel Verneuil €€€ *8 rue de Verneuil, 75007, tel: 01 42 60 82 14, fax: 01 42 61 40 38, <www.hotelverneuil.com>*. Lovely hotel in an elegant 17th-century building in the upmarket 7th *arrondissement*, with small but attractive rooms in the traditional style. Discreet service. Singer Serge Gainsbourg lived on this street, and the wall outside his old house is decorated with graffiti in homage. Well placed for St-Germain.

MONTPARNASSE

Hôtel Aviatic €€ *105 rue de Vaugirard, tel: 01 53 63 25 50, fax: 01 53 63 25 55, <www.aviatic.fr>*. A comfortable small hotel on a pleasant street not far from the Luxembourg Gardens. The bedrooms have been recently refurbished, and there is a charming breakfast room and Empire-style lounge. Worth upgrading to a superior room, if your budget allows.

Recommended Restaurants

In this section we cover cafés, bistros and brasseries. Generally speaking, restaurants serve lunch from noon–2.30 or 3pm and dinner from around 7 or 8–10.30 or 11pm, although this may vary. If you wish to dine particularly early or late, ask your hotel's concierge to call to confirm a restaurant's hours of operation. Opening and closing times can vary, particularly in August, when many establishments shut for the summer.

The price ranges quoted below (given as a guide only) are per person for a three-course dinner with a glass of house wine and tax and service included. Extras will send bills much higher; conversely, a modest lunch menu, especially a *prixe-fixe* formula, can cost considerably less.

€€€€	over 80 euros
€€€	50–80 euros
€€	30–50 euros
€	below 30 euros

THE RIGHT BANK

LOUVRE AND TUILERIES

Café Marly €€–€€€ *Palais du Louvre, 93 rue de Rivoli, 75001, tel: 01 49 26 06 60.* Open daily for lunch and dinner (until 2am). Rest from your labours at the Louvre in the lavish Second Empire-style rooms facing the Pyramid or on the attractive covered terrace. This café is popular with the fashionable set and tends to be busy. Modern European cooking. Nice for breakfast.

Costes €€€€ *239 rue St-Honoré, 75001, tel: 01 42 44 50 25.* Open daily 7am–1am. This restaurant in the chic Hotel Costes is one of the most popular upmarket venues in Paris. Beautiful courtyard and a baroque interior with crystal chandeliers. Eclectic menu. Reserve.

Le Fumoir €€–€€€ *6 rue de l'Amiral-de-Coligny, 75001, tel: 01 42 92 00 24.* Open daily for lunch and dinner; brunch on Sunday. With an admirable location facing the Louvre, spacious, sophisticated Le Fumoir is renowned for shaking some of the best cocktails in town. It serves light pan-European cooking, such as monkfish with peas and asparagus and sea bass with ginger.

Le Grand Véfour €€€€ *17 rue de Beaujolais, 75001, tel: 01 42 96 56 27.* Open Mon–Fri for lunch, Mon–Thurs for dinner. Set under the arches of the Palais-Royal is one of the most beautiful restaurants in Paris. Le Grand Véfour opened its doors in 1784 and has fed the likes of Emperor Napoléon and writers Alphonse Lamartine and Victor Hugo. Today it serves haute cuisine in the hands of chef Guy Martin.

GRANDS BOULEVARDS

Alain Ducasse au Plaza Athénée €€€€ *25 avenue Montaigne, 75008, tel: 01 53 67 65 00.* Open for lunch Thurs–Fri, dinner Mon–Fri. Cooking elevated to an art form from France's first recipient of six Michelin stars (three apiece for two restaurants), in the hands of his acolyte Christophe Moret. According to globetrotting chef Alain Ducasse, his meals are not about fancy presentation but purity and essence of flavour. Expect truffles in abundance but also superb vegetables from Provence, where Ducasse first made his name. The listed neo-rococo decor has been rejuvenated with a shower of ethereal glittery crystals. Reserve well ahead.

Angl'Opéra €€€ *39 avenue de l'Opéra, 75008, tel: 01 42 61 86 25.* Michelin-starred chef Gilles Choukroun turns out daring, but delicious, creations in the funky restaurant of the Hôtel Edouard VII *(see page 130).* A good choice if you've overdosed on traditional French fare.

Café de la Paix €€–€€€ *place de l'Opéra, 75009, tel: 01 40 07 36 36.* The main reason to come here is the historic setting of this 1862 café; it's vast, gilded and mirrored, adjoining a covered terrace opposite the Palais Garnier.

Chartier € *7 rue du Faubourg-Montmartre, 75009, tel: 01 47 70 86 29.* Open all day Mon–Sat. The best-known low-price eatery in town. The ambience is an experience in itself: Belle Epoque decor, snappy waiters, shared tables and plenty of *bonhomie*. Arrive before 1pm or before 8pm at night or you may not get a seat.

Gallopin €€€ *40 rue Notre-Dame-des-Victoires 75002, tel: 01 42 36 45 38.* Open for lunch and dinner Mon–Sat. This famous brasserie opposite the Stock Exchange opened in 1876 and is still decorated in elegant Belle Epoque style. The chef prepares refined versions of traditional dishes, including *pâté maison*, grilled meats and flambéed *crêpes*. The fish is a star attraction, with specialities such as haddock poached in milk with fresh spinach, and deliciously fresh seafood platters. Delightful food in a gorgeous setting.

Ladurée €€ *75 avenue des Champs-Elysées, 75008, tel: 01 40 75 08 75.* Open daily 8am–1am. Renowned in Paris for generations for its delectable macaroons, this café/bakery/restaurant is always busy and very chic. Excellent puff pastry filled with veal and mushrooms, and baked cod with candied lemon. Desserts are a particular strength, especially the melt-in-the-mouth macaroons. There's also a branch at 16 rue Royale.

Spoon €€ *14 rue de Marignan 75008, tel: 01 40 76 34 44.* Open weekdays for lunch and dinner. The prototype of Ducasse's mix-and-match global kitchens draws a hot mix of media, fashion and showbiz types. The restaurant has two personalities, as white linen shades on the dining room walls are raised in the evening to reveal purple upholstered walls. Desserts are often of American inspiration. Book ahead.

CHAMPS-ELYSEES AND TROCADÉRO

L'Appart €€–€€€ *9–11 rue du Colisée, 75008, tel: 01 53 75 42 00.* Open daily for lunch and dinner; Sunday brunch. Close to the Champs-Elysées, this modern bistro looks more like someone's apartment (hence the name) with shelves of books lining the walls. The cooking is creative but not fussy: think colourful salads, candied aubergine, veal with mustard seeds, and fresh cod with mashed potatoes. Reasonably priced wines.

Tokyo Eat €€ *Palais de Tokyo, 13 avenue du Président Wilson, 75016, tel: 01 47 20 00 29.* Open for lunch and dinner Tues–Sun An airy space with open kitchen and funky lighting. The menu skips from global satays and unusual carpaccios to roast chicken. The terrace is open in summer.

BEAUBOURG, MARAIS, BASTILLE AND EAST

L'Apparement Café € *18 rue des Coutures-St-Gervais, 75003, tel: 01 48 87 12 22.* Stepping inside this quaint café near the Musée Picasso is like entering someone's house. Cosy seats make for lovely lazy dining, and simple, tasty food. There are board games, too.

L'As du Fallafel € *34 rue des Rosiers, 75004, tel: 01 48 87 63 60.* Open Sun–Fri noon–midnight, closed Sat. The best *falafel* in Paris is a meal in itself. There are also *shawarma* sandwiches in pitta bread. Great location in the heart of the Marais.

Brasserie Bofinger €€–€€€ *5–7 rue de la Bastille, 75004, tel: 01 42 72 87 82.* Open daily for lunch and dinner. Close to the Opéra Bastille, the huge (300-seater) Bofinger is the archetypal Belle Epoque brasserie, complete with lush red-and-gold decor. It's a great place in which to experience brasserie fare: delicious oysters and seafood and specialities from Alsace such as *choucroute*. Excellent service.

Chai 33 €€–€€€ *33 cour St-Emilion, 75012, tel: 01 53 44 01 01.* Innovative restaurant set in a light, airy former wine warehouse in hip Bercy. Choose your wine according to six styles, from light with a bite to rich and silky, with refreshing fusion food to match. Unpretentious *sommeliers* are on hand to help with wine choices. Fun.

Chez Prune €–€€ *71 quai Valmy, 75010, tel: 01 42 41 30 47.* Open daily for lunch and dinner. A cornerstone of the trendy Canal St-Martin area. This is still one of the better places in Paris from which to watch the world go by. Good food at lunchtime; tapas-style snacks at night.

Le Petit Fer à Cheval € *30 rue Vieille-du-Temple, 75004, tel: 01 42 72 47 47.* Open daily for lunch and dinner. People-watching is as much a full-time occupation here as it is anywhere else along the Marais's trendy rue Vieille-du-Temple. With its tiny horseshoe-shaped bar, this café is atmospheric and a great favourite with the bourgeois-bohemian crowd. Decent food. Friendly service.

Le Petit Marcel €–€€ *65 rue Rambuteau, 75004, tel: 01 48 87 10 20.* Open daily for lunch and dinner (until 12am). This formerly postage stamp-sized bistro – now expanded – near the Centre Pompidou is as quaint as it gets, with attractive Art Nouveau tiles. The locals will grab the few terrace seats first, but inside, beneath the painted ceiling on a rickety chair, you're just as much part of the scene. Salads, omelettes, steak frites, tarte Tatin: basic food, but decent, cheap and delightful. No credit cards.

Le Square Trousseau €€–€€€ *1 rue Antoine-Vollon, 75012, tel: 01 43 43 06 00.* Open Tues–Sat for lunch and dinner. It's no surprise that this bistro has been used for film sets: inside it's spacious, with Art Deco lamps, colourful tiles and a glamorous bar. In summer, diners squeeze on to the terrace facing a leafy square. Gazpacho, tuna tartare, rosemary lamb and spring vegetables, beef with shallot sauce, and raspberry gratin are among the delights available.

Train Bleu €€ *Gare de Lyon, 750012, tel: 01 43 43 09 06.* Open daily for lunch and dinner. Built over a century ago in the midst of the Gare de Lyon, this huge, lavish-looking restaurant is considered an artistic marvel, with frescoed ceilings, mosaics and Belle Epoque murals. Classic French dishes are served quickly and efficiently. Good-value set menus.

WESTERN PARIS

Guy Savoy €€€€ *18 rue Troyon, 75017, tel: 01 43 80 40 61.* Open for lunch Tues–Fri, dinner Tues–Sat. It took some time for Savoy's imaginative haute cuisine to finally earn the highest Michelin rating, belated recognition of one of Paris's most inventive chefs. The son of a gardener, Savoy has an obsession with vegetables that anticipated the recent trend by more than a decade. He happily pairs truffles with lentils or artichokes, and regularly makes the rounds to greet his guests.

Pré Catelan €€€€ *route de Suresnes, 75016, tel: 01 44 14 41 14*. Open for lunch and dinner Tues–Sat, lunch only on Sun. Situated in the heart of the Bois de Boulogne, this is one of the most romantic spots in Paris. Haute cuisine centring on fresh truffles, lobster, lamb and fresh seafood. The pastry chef is considered one of the best in France. Call well ahead to book a table.

MONTMARTRE AND THE NORTHEAST

Au Grain de Folie € *24 rue de la Vieuville, 75018, tel: 01 42 58 15 57*. Open for lunch and dinner Mon–Sat, non-stop Sun 12.30–11pm. A self-styled 'vegetarian place for non-vegetarians', this is a quaint spot for a healthy bite on your way to the Butte. Sit at a check-cloth-covered table, among the cooking implements and pot plants, and enjoy a bowl of homemade soup, a crispy vegetable platter, or a slice of savoury tart. A tight squeeze but friendly atmosphere.

Casa Olympe €€ *48 rue St-Georges, 75009, tel: 01 42 85 26 01*. Open Mon–Fri for lunch and dinner (closed first three weeks in Aug). Olympe Versini is one of Paris's best-known female chefs, and in this no-frills dining room she offers a limited but strong menu. Classic French dishes such as *steak tartare* hit the spot.

THE RIGHT BANK

LATIN QUARTER AND ST-GERMAIN-DES-PRÉS

L'Alcazar €€–€€€ *62 rue Mazarine, 75006, tel: 01 53 10 19 99*. Open daily for lunch and dinner, brunch on Sun. Sir Terence Conran's contribution to the Paris restaurant scene was to transform this former musical hall into a designer brasserie. It's been a hit, thanks to the easygoing atmosphere and competitively priced menu, which includes an upmarket interpretation of British fish and chips.

Allard €€–€€€ *41 rue St-André des Arts, 75006, tel: 01 43 26 48 23*. The dark, Art Nouveau decoration makes this one of the loveliest bistros in Paris, with two small but intimate and atmospheric rooms evocative of Left Bank life. The traditional food – think duck with olives, roasted lamb, etc – is very good.

Angelina's €€–€€€ *226 rue de Rivoli, 75001, tel: 01 42 60 82 00*. Famed Paris tearoom that is also good for lunch. Serves great squishy meringues.

Brasserie Lipp €€–€€€ *151 boulevard St-Germain, 75006, tel: 01 45 48 53 91*. Open daily for lunch and dinner until 1am. Everyone who's anyone in St-Germain-des-Prés has a table here. Not to be missed for a view of the neighbourhood eccentrics. Brasserie fare (Alsace country cooking), notably stews and *choucroute* (sauerkraut). Reasonably priced house Riesling.

La Closerie des Lilas €€–€€€ *171 boulevard du Montparnasse, 75006, tel: 01 40 51 34 50*. Open daily for lunch and dinner. Spiritual home to Left Bank intellectuals, the Closerie remains one of the most attractive institutions in the city. There's a reliable brasserie, a more expensive restaurant (great French classics) and a lovely bar.

Polidor € *41 rue Monsieur-le-Prince, 75006, tel: 01 43 26 95 34*. Open daily for lunch and dinner. This bohemian restaurant is a perennial favourite of students and budget diners. The *plats du jour* have been reliable for around 150 years and arrive in hearty helpings. Blood sausage with mash and rice pudding are just the kind of stodgy dishes to expect. Great value for money.

AROUND THE EIFFEL TOWER

L'Atelier de Joël Robuchon €€€€ *5 rue Montalembert, 75007, tel: 01 42 22 56 56*. Open daily for lunch and dinner. Even jaded Parisians queue up in all weathers to sample the warm *foie gras brochettes* or tapenade with fresh tuna conjured by France's most revered chef. The restaurant is built around an open kitchen, so you can watch the masters at work, and the atmosphere is slick, like that of a bar. Reservations are accepted for first seatings only (11.30am and 6.30pm). No smoking.

Au Bon Accueil €€–€€€ *14 rue de Monttessuy, 75007, tel: 01 47 05 46 11.* Open Mon–Fri for lunch and dinner. What was once a Provençal bistro has been given a total makeover – the décor is now sleek contemporary and elegant, and the menu of classics has been modernised as well. The prix-fixe dinner menu (around €30) is viewed by many locals as one of the best deals in the neighbourhood, and the wine list is excellent. Seats on the terrace have views of the Eiffel Tower.

Le Jules Verne €€€€ *2nd floor, Eiffel Tower, 75007, tel: 01 45 55 61 44.* Open daily for lunch and dinner. Location-wise, this restaurant on the second level of the Eiffel Tower is perfect for a celebration or romantic dinner, though the cooking is not quite as spectacular as the view. Specialities include a *tartare duo* (beef and langoustine), *noix de St-Jacques* (scallops) and *crêpes* with Grand Marnier. One for a special occasion.

MONTPARNASSE

La Closerie des Lilas €€ *171 boulevard du Montparnasse, 75006, tel: 01 40 51 34 50.* Open daily for lunch and dinner. The brasserie still has a lot of charm and richly satisfying fare, though it lives off its reputation as a watering hole in the 1920s – tables are inscribed with the names of clients Lenin, Modigliani and Surrealist poet André Breton. Fittingly, Hemingway's plaque rests on the bar. A pianist plays in the evening. Skip the overpriced restaurant annex.

La Coupole €€–€€€ *102 boulevard du Montparnasse, 75014, tel: 01 43 20 14 20.* This vast, iconic Art Deco brasserie – the largest in Paris – is still going strong, and has been since 1927. Now run by the Flo Brasserie group, its buzzing atmosphere and popularity remain intact. Brasserie fare includes huge platters of shellfish and grilled meats.

INDEX

Berlitz pocket guide

Paris

Fifteenth Edition 2008

Written by Martin Gostelow
Updated by Simon Cropper
Series Editor: Tony Halliday

Printed in Singapore by Insight Print Services (Pte) Ltd, 38 Joo Koon Road, Singapore 628990. Tel: (65) 6865-1600. Fax: (65) 6861-6438

Berlitz Trademark Reg. U.S. Patent Office and other countries. Marca Registrada

Photography credits
AKG London 18, 58; Apa 79; The Art Archive 36, 74, 87; The Art Archive/ Musée du Louvre 37; Pete Bennett 51, 84; Corbis 22, 80; Jerry Dennis 6, 8, 16, 25, 26, 27, 28, 30, 31, 34, 39, 43, 47, 57, 60, 62, 63, 65, 67, 68, 70, 72, 75, 77, 83, 85, 96; Annabel Elston 12, 56, 69; Courtesy of the French Embassy 20, 22; Jay Fechtman 15, 24; Francisco Hidalgo/Getty 33; Britta Jaschinski 9, 10, 38, 40, 42, 44, 45, 48, 49, 50, 52, 54, 66, 76, 88, 90, 91, 92, 98, 101, 102, 103, 104; Musée Association Les Amis d'Edith Piaf 95; Ilpo Musto 46

Cover picture: Ary Diesendruck/Getty Images

Contact us

At Berlitz we strive to keep our guides as accurate and up to date as possible, but if you find anything that has changed, or if you have any suggestions on ways to improve this guide, then we would be delighted to hear from you.

Berlitz Publishing, PO Box 7910, London SE1 1WE, England.
fax: (44) 20 7403 0290
email: berlitz@apaguide.co.uk
www.berlitzpublishing.com